CHINA
AND THE WEST

A CARAVAN UNDER THE WALLS OF PEKING

CHINA
AND THE WEST

A SHORT HISTORY OF THEIR CONTACT
FROM ANCIENT TIMES TO THE
FALL OF THE MANCHU DYNASTY

William Edward Soothill

WESTHOLME
Yardley

that there was early contact between China and nations to the westward. There are points of affinity with other races and hints of borrowed or introduced elements of early civilization, which suggest that Chinese development has not been independent of external influences. For instance, the knowledge of astronomy which faces us in the earliest known period gives the impression of something not indigenous. Whether there is any direct connection between the pictographs of the Sumerians and those of the Chinese awaits the investigation of a competent Sino-Assyriologist, who perhaps may yet be a thoroughly trained Chinese.

Whatever may be said of those prehistoric times, it is a mistake to assume, as is so commonly assumed, that foreign intercourse is a comparatively modern experience with the Chinese. They are generally supposed to have been so shut in by Himalayas, or high mountains of one sort or another, by deserts, by the Pacific Ocean and especially by the Great Wall, that they have had no contact and no desire for contact with the outside world. It was a land sealed to the world, ' the world' of course meaning Europe, or rather a small part of Europe. The parochial way in which too many Europeans still speak of ' the world ' reminds one of the man who said that Christianity was responsible for all the evil and half the good in the world, though it is still unknown to the masses of Asia and Africa, where nevertheless there is much evil and much good.

China may indeed have known nothing of Europe until about the time that Europe learned something about China; but, of many things, one is certain, that the Chinese from the beginning of their history had foreign intercourse of a strenuous character. True, the foreigners were not those who came on to the scene at a very modern date, Portuguese, Spaniards, Dutch, British, Italians, French, Russians, Germans, least of all Americans, for in those early days this conglomeration of adventuring people did not exist as nations, and had not yet begun to dispute over their meagre possessions. At that time the only foreigners known to the Chinese were the other mongoloid tribes over whom, by some quality of superior intelligence, they obtained the mastery. The struggle was long and often fierce, for the hunter-fisherman resisted and still resists the invasion of his hunting grounds by the ever encroaching 'foreign' farmer. By degrees the superior race prevailed over their unlettered inferiors and drove them to the mountain fastnesses, or absorbed them and turned them into Chinese.

It is manifest that the Chinese are not now a single tribe, or even the supposed original 'hundred clans' of which their early history composes them. What the names of those 'hundred clans' were is not now known; but a comparatively late list containing four hundred single and thirty double clan names, styled 'The hundred family surnames,' has been an elementary school-book

for centuries and only recently been superseded.
In the West we have nothing like it outside the
twelve tribes or clans of Israel.   Imagine the surnames of all the Norman barons and knights being
an elementary school-book with us !   Or even
the Highland schoolboy committing to memory,
as one of his earliest series of lessons, a complete
list of the Scottish clans !   That is what Chinese
children did, those who went to school, of number
proportionately few, and this they did though the
great majority of the children did not find their
own names among them.   The surnames of
China to-day are certainly more than two thousand in number.   The surmise therefore is not
unreasonable that the ' hundred clans ' or surnames represent the hundred tribes who formed
the original alliance which forced its primitive
but growing culture on surrounding inferior
tribes, and that the two thousand and more
surnames found to-day are for the most part
those of tribes that have been brought from
the condition of foreigners and opponents
into the family of which we call the Chinese
nation.

In brief, then, the Chinese may be described
as a great admixture of similar racial tribes, a
mixture which is not yet ended but still proceeding, and which will proceed further as the
farmer continues to absorb the hunter-fisherman
on the one hand and the herdsman on the other.
In the Western world there is still in progress a

remarkable mixing of Western breeds, especially in America, an admixture of which no one can see the end. Similarly will there be further admixture in the East. The original dominant Chinese stock no longer has a separate existence. Cross-fertilization has been at work for thousands of years, perhaps to the advantage of the race, for cross-fertilization within the same race is generally counted as healthy. In passing it may be remarked that, as yet, there is no evidence that among widely different races it may not also be healthy, when cultural conditions more nearly converge.

Even after the early absorption of their immediate neighbours the Chinese did not find an empty world. It was true five thousand years ago, as it is to-day, that the wider the circle was expanded the more were its points of human and racial contact. Thus, expansion in course of time found the Chinese confronting the most terrible of their foes, foes it is true of their own racial type, but the fiercest foes in all Asia and later the terror of Europe. It was one thing to subjugate tribes of surrounding hunter-fishermen ; it was quite another to come into contact with the fierce herdsman, who could ride swift and deep into one's territory and slaughter, raid, burn and retreat at will. The savage Hsiung-nu, or Hun, found in the agricultural Chinese encroachers to be distrusted and suppressed. Undoubtedly he could exchange his sheep, cattle and furs for the grain, linen and silks of the settler, but—it was pleasanter to raid him.

It will be realized then that the Chinese had early experience of ' foreigners ' of their own racial type, long before they came into contact with other races. As long as they were successful in absorbing weaker tribes, there was no anti-foreign feeling. Such feeling naturally began to crystallize when they were the victims and not the victors. At any rate they early learnt the value and even the sanctity of treaties. Through two thousand years wars and treaties alternated, neither side having more to its credit than the other in the observance of those treaties, though on both sides there are conspicuous instances of a high sense of honour in regard to them.

The Great Wall is one of the clearest indications of the character of China's early foreign relations. Nor was it valueless in its aim of fending off the Huns, or of dividing them from and preventing their alliance with other troublesome races in the north-west. The Huns, ferocious horsemen, unable to ride over or through it, were deflected by it and its defenders westward, where at a later period they made the solid earth shake under their myriad savage hoofs and caused even the peoples of Western Europe to fear and quake.

The now famous centres of Tun-huang, Lou-lan, and the series of garrisons along the line of the Great Wall in Central Asia bear witness of another kind. These and other endeavours give evidence not only of China's devices for self-protection, but of a desire to open and keep open a way to the West.   Founded in B.C. 111 as a stronghold and a city for the protection of travellers and merchants, as well as for the defence of the frontier, Tun-huang fell into ruins five centuries ago.   This and other sand-buried garrisons have yielded up invaluable treasures to Sir Aurel Stein of records dating from the first century B.C.

To deal, however, with China's ancient and mediæval intercourse with all external peoples would cover more ground than would be of interest to the ordinary reader.   It would include intercourse with Tibet, Turkestan, Mongolia, Manchuria, Korea, Japan, Burma, Annam, Siam, India ; indeed all the countries bordering on the Central Empire.   The purpose of this book is rather to consider the intercourse which has led the Chinese into contact with Occidental nations.

II

FOREIGN INTERCOURSE BEFORE THE MONGOL
CONQUEST OF CHINA

WE do not know when China first met the Occident. We do not even know much about its first acquaintance with the tribes and peoples on its far western, or Central Asian borders. It is, however, quite clear that there was intercourse before our era. Probably the earliest cause of Occidental interest was the lure of silk. The Land of the Seres is one of the earliest names by which China was known to the West. Ssu, pronounced *sz*, is the Chinese name as *ser* is the Mongolian name for silk, and evidently the latter name accompanied the product into Greece and Rome. Virgil, Horace, Strabo, Pomponius Mela, Pliny the Elder, all speak of the Seres, or of the Sericae. Silk was the lure that sent men along the route spoken of by Ptolemy, via Hierapolis, along the Euphrates, by Hekatompylos, Aria and Margiana (Merv) to Bactria, thence past the Oxus to Kashgar and Ferghana. There they apparently found the market for silks from China and other articles of commerce.

Though such intercourse may have lasted for

a long period, and there are certain early indications of it in Chinese records, China only became officially aware of a Western world about B.C. 150. Even then the knowledge was only of Western Asia and not of Europe.   In or about the year B.C. 138, the intrepid Chinese general Chang Ch'ien, who by his exploits earned the name of ' Road-opener,' set out from the court of the Emperor Wu of the Han dynasty on the first official mission to the West.

The mission was political rather than one of discovery.   A tribe of Indo-Scythians had for long inhabited a territory now part of the Chinese north-west province of Kansu.   Harried by the Huns, its ruler slain and his skull turned into a Hun drinking-cup, the Yue-chi decided to seek a home less open to depredation.   In one of those mass movements which brought change in its train to the whole of Asia, the Yue-chi abandoned their territory and pushed westward to the territory of the Wu-sun, then to that of the Saka tribe.   These it dispossessed of their lands and they in their turn dispossessed other tribes in India, where the Sakas settled.   The process was similar to that which was occurring in Europe, which continued through much of European history, and which is being repeated in America, Australia and Africa.

The Yue-chi are by some considered to be the Getae of the Greeks.   It has been suggested Yut, the original sound of Yue, is the Chinese

representation of ' Get,' the same as the Indian
Jāt. Professor Parker says that an early pronunciation of Yue-chi was Yeh-t'a, or Yi-t'a,
allying the race to that of Ephthah, or the Eph-
thalites. By some it is thought that they are the
ancestors of, or of the same race with the Turks,
at any rate that they are originally identical or
parallel developments of the same tribe. The
Saka or Shaka were the Sacae or Sakai of classical
authors. ' The name and original nomadic life
are points in common ' with the Scythians, but
Sir Charles Eliot thinks ' they cannot be the same
as the Scythians of Europe.'

Returning to the Yue-chi of Kansu, it is
evident that the Emperor of China, while sym-
pathizing with their frequent sufferings, felt even
more that he had lost a useful people to act as a
buffer state between his nation and the Huns,
or as a barrier preventing the junction of the
northern Huns with warlike tribes to their southward. Be that as it may, he sent off General
Chang, whose name, like most of the Changs of
China, might be translated Bowman, or Archer.
The general, with a hundred chosen followers,
was commissioned to discover the whereabouts
of the Yue-chi, and empowered to induce them to
return to their old abode under the guarantee of
China's co-operation and protection. On the way
the mission fell into the hands of the Huns.
These apparently did not treat its leader harshly,
but detained him strictly. In order to disarm

suspicion he settled down cheerfully among them, marrying a wife and having a son. Ten long years, never forgetting his mission, he awaited his opportunity to escape. At last, while the tribe of his captors were busily engaged against another tribe, he succeeded in fleeing accompanied by one of his hundred followers. Making his way westward, after an adventurous journey, he at last found the Yue-chi. His discovery was too late. Bactria had proved to them a territory more attractive than Kansu and, free from the harassings of the Huns, they were now too comfortably ensconced to return.

It may here be pointed out that from this people, the Yue-chi, sprang Kanishka, the great Scythian protector and propagator of Buddhism about the beginning of our era. His kingdom stretched southward as far as Madura in India and north-west to Bokhara. ' The reign of Kanishka was certainly the turning point' in fixing Sanskrit as the written language of India, and this was ' partly the cause, partly the effect of a complete revulsion in the intellectual life of India.' A senior contemporary of Kanishka's was As'vagosha, the virtual founder of Mahayana Buddhism, which later became the form prevalent in China.

To a migration of nomad hordes was due in part the downfall of the Roman civilization. ' It was the migration of nomad hordes that led, in India, to the downfall of the Buddhist civilization, and subsequently, after the conversion of the Saka and Tartar invaders, to the development of mediæval Hinduism.'

General Chang had the spirit of the explorer and would have pushed further westward in his endeavour to know what was beyond the beyond ; but duty to his sovereign bade him return, so reluctantly he turned his feet homeward. His furthest point westward was Bokhara, the region between the Jaxartes and the Oxus. While at Ferghana he noticed Chinese bamboo work and other articles from China for sale. His curiosity was aroused as to the route they had followed to so distant a mart. Enquiries showed him that there existed regular communication between South-west China, India and Central Asia. Evidently this route proceeded still further westward. He mentions three routes from China to the West—via Tibet, which he describes as extremely hazardous ; via the north-west route, with almost certain capture by the Huns ; and via Szechwan and Yunnan as by far the safest.

Setting out on his perilous return journey, he was intercepted by another Tartar tribe, who held him prisoner for a year, when he again succeeded in escaping. After an absence of between thirteen and fourteen years he reached his master's court, with only his faithful companion left of the original hundred followers. To the emperor he gave a full account of his travels, experiences and observations, which were duly recorded and are still extant.   Unlike Marco Polo, who on his return was considered to be a romancer, General Chang was welcomed, believed and rewarded with high position.   He brought back with him—no doubt hidden as seeds in his clothing—the walnut, the grape and hemp, which are a perpetual monument in China to his memory.   He was again entrusted with plenipotentiary powers, and by B.C. 115 had entered into treaties with thirty-six external states.

As Sir Aurel Stein has said: ' The intercourse of which he had been the pioneer rapidly developed and increased, until embassies attended by several hundred men, we are told, " followed upon one another's heels all along the route." From the account we receive of certain abuses which before long came to attend these missions to distant foreign lands, we may conclude that in many cases they were largely prompted or exploited by private commercial enterprise.   We may, in fact, surmise that these " embassies " were often but a counterpart of those trading caravans from the West, which the Chinese court, during the Middle Ages and later, prided themselves upon receiving under the guise of tribute-bearing missions.   And the same probability holds good also of that " coming and going of ambassadors of the foreign countries of the northwest," which after the first opening of intercourse by Chang Ch'ien is said to have become more and more frequent.'

Measures for the protection of the border, meant at the outset to be chiefly prohibitive of external intercourse, led on the contrary to its expansion. The development of trade brought with it the need for the ever advancing protection of the trade routes. With this came ever widening political relations, so that China was gradually drawn further and further afield by its traders—as has been the case with Great Britain—until its responsibilities ultimately extended far westward into Asia.

So rapid was this early expansion that by B.C. 104 it became necessary to avenge the murder of Chinese envoys at Ferghana, and General Li Kuang-li was sent with a large force on this punitive expedition; but, the terrible desert and salt-marsh exhausting his troops, he was defeated and only about a tenth of his force returned alive. In 102 he was again on the march with sixty thousand men and better supplies. ' This time Chinese powers of intelligent organization triumphed over all the difficulties of nature, almost insuperable' in 'the forbidding desert which it had to cross between Tun-huang and Lou-lan' —so says Sir Aurel Stein, who of all men knows its hardships. General Li was as successful in arms as in organization; Ferghana submitted and Chinese prestige became widely acknowledged.

Traffic across the desert greatly increased, with consequent interchange of commodities east and west, as well as an interchange of ideas. The tribes along the route, protected by the Chinese against the Huns, became subject to China and intermediaries with the regions beyond. When later the power of the Hun emperors waned, it was restored, towards the end of the first century A.D., by General Pan Ch'ao, ' the greatest of the soldier statesmen who ever served China's Central-Asian policy.' His conquests extended far to the west, beyond the Pamirs ; he entered into diplomatic relations with Parthia, and sent an envoy, Kan Ying, to Ta Ts'in, the Syrian border of the Roman empire. Kan Ying reached the Persian Gulf, but was deterred—or his companions were—by the reported perils of the way ; probably equally by ignorance of the language and the jealousy of monopolising traders.

It was, no doubt, a considerable time before the period of Chang Ch'ien that China became known further west by that name. The Chinese have never themselves so styled their country. There is little doubt that the name China originated from the feudal state of Ts'in, the nearest state to the West. That state was powerful as early as the eighth century B.C., and its latest baron, in B.C. 255, finally subdued his fellow-barons, became the *soi-disant* ' First Emperor ' and laid the foundation of China's unity and imperial government. Ts'in, Tsinitza, Tzinista, Sinim, Sinae, Thinae, Cinasthana, Cinistan, China, Chine—these, with the doubtful exception of Sinim, are almost certainly derivatives of

Ts'in, the far western Chinese state, which passed on its name, possibly through the Yue-chi, to the West, long before the last of its barons unified China under the short-lived Ts'in dynasty.

As already mentioned, China had been known in the West by its product of silk. As Seres it was known to the Greeks and Romans, possibly first through Parthia and the Persians, then through the Alexandrian conquests. It may be that individual Chinese merchants reached Rome before the Christian era. Certainly men of their colour were known to the West. They seem to have reached Alexandria at an early date and were undoubtedly known in Parthia, but the records, east and west, throw little light on the subject. Chinese history notes the arrival in China in A.D. 196 of an envoy from the Emperor Antonine (Marcus Aurelius), but he may only have been a Syrian merchant. Hindu envoys are recorded in A.D. 159 and 161, and there is previous mention as early as B.C. 89 and 105. About A.D. 164 an astronomical treatise is reported to have reached China from the Roman empire, but that empire to the Chinese was, or began in Persia, so the treatise may have been Persian.

It was thus the impact of the Huns, the age-long enemies of China, of Asia and of Europe, which drove westward the Yue-chi into Bactria, where they remained until they were swept along by the Hun whirlwind to carry devastation upon the Roman empire. In their first western migration, the Yue-chi pushed away the Sakas (Sacae), who in turn pressed into India, founded an empire on the ruins of that of Sandracottas (Candragupta) and As'oka and ultimately drove the Greeks out of India; but not before that wonderful people had left, amongst other things, its artistic impress on that region, an impress which influenced the whole of Buddhist art throughout China and the Far East as well as in India.

We know then that from the period of General Chang Ch'ien the Chinese became officially cognizant of Central and Western Asia. Another consequence of Chang Ch'ien's explorations was the endeavour to open the south-western passage to India. The result of this was the entering into relations with the Burmese tribes in what is now South-west China, and, centuries later, the conquest of Burma.

From these endeavours it may reasonably be asserted that the Chinese were not originally averse from international relations; but rather welcomed intercourse with other peoples, indeed sought it, as is shown especially by their efforts to penetrate westward, and soon after the days of Chang Ch'ien by the deliberate imperial introduction of Buddhism into China. M. Pelliot is of opinion that early in the first century of our era a Chinese mission crossed the Indian Ocean. At any rate, it is manifest that China was not then the walled-in foreign-hating country that it has seemed to be.

III

BUDDHISTS, ARABS, CHRISTIANS AND OTHERS, BEFORE THE MONGOL INVASION

BEFORE the days of Chang Ch'ien, Buddhism in some form or another seems to have filtered into the north-west of China, through Yue-chi channels. The year A.D. 67—though some put the date as early as B.C. 2—has generally been considered as that in which Buddhism was formally introduced at and by the court of China. The records, the authenticity of which are somewhat in doubt, state that Indian monks were received and employed by the emperor, these being the earliest representatives of an alien religion and an alien culture.

The influence of this impact of West on East —for India and Central Asia were ' the West ' to the Chinese of those days—and the consequent reaction of East on West, were of much importance to world relations. It is a subject which has not even yet been sufficiently elucidated. As to the East the fertilization of Chinese thought through Buddhism was not limited to religion. In that respect alone it powerfully affected Chinese character and even more that of the

barbaric tribes on the north and west. Buddhism
reached China before Confucianism and Taoism
were finally differentiated into separate cults, and
while Chinese philosophy was groping its way
towards a clearer definition.   At this fluid period,
Buddhism brought an element into Chinese life
which soon precipitated the thoughts in solution,
and crystallized them into the philosophies and
cults known as Confucianism, Taoism, and
Buddhism, commonly spoken of as ' The Three
Religions.'

The form of Buddhism which reached China
was that of the ' northern ' school, which developed into the Mahayana, or Universalist cult,
though the ideas and scriptures of the Hinayana,
or what might be called the Orthodox school,
were also accepted.   In brief, the distinguishing
principles of Mahayanism are : 1. an Ultimate
Buddha, who manifests himself at rare intervals
in an earthly vehicle, resembling somewhat the
Greek Logos : Gautama, or Sakyamuni Buddha,
is his latest incarnation ; 2. the Ultimate Buddha
is in every man and being, and every man and
being is Buddha ; 3. therefore there is final
salvation for all ; 4. such salvation may be
immediate through faith or invocation, or it may
be through many purifications, including all kinds
of reincarnations, purgatories, hells, and even
Brahma heavens, for the gods are also mortal ;
5. an ultimate heaven, which is not a semi-material
or Brahma heaven, but a pure, formless or

spiritual and immortal Buddha heaven. In the most popular Mahayana cult, the salvation by works taught by Sakymuni in the flesh, and by the 'southern,' or Hinayana school, is transformed, through 'a final revelation,' into salvation by faith in and by invocation of Bodhisattvas, *i.e.* saints or saviours who have vowed to help and save all living beings. Among such are Amitabha, Kuan-yin (the so-called Goddess of Mercy) and many others. This form of Buddhism, so different from the orthodox school, seems to have resulted from Persian importations, and not, as sometimes suggested, to have been influenced by Christian doctrines.

Other Indian ideas were introduced to the considerable enrichment of Chinese culture. Graeco-Bactrian art, especially in the form of sculpture, was imported probably direct from Central Asia, though later from India. That Indian sculpture was largely influenced by the Greek spirit is generally recognized ; the invasion of India by Alexander and the establishment of the Seleucids in Persia and Western India having left there definite Greek characteristics. Sculpture obtained a freedom and power hitherto unknown, which took possession of Chinese sculptural art when introduced by the Buddhists. The mighty rock carvings in Shansi, the huge Buddhas at Lung-men in Honan which are far larger than the famous Kamakura image in Japan, the Kamakura image itself, and the millions of images in China, Mongolia, Manchuria, Tibet, Korea, Japan and the whole of the Far East, are the result of this intercourse between West and East.

Again, Western letters at a later date became the foundation of the literature of Tibet, Mongolia and Manchuria, but the existing written system of China and its literature were too firmly enthroned to be shaken by so slight a thing as an alphabet. Some may consider this to be one of the greatest misfortunes that China has suffered, as an alphabet would have given the people a more flexible medium of expression, and greatly increased the number of readers, with consequent intellectual development and enrichment. There is, however, another point of view, for it is doubtful if China would have maintained its homogeneity on a phonetic basis, and after all it is the eye which reads and not the ear ! One of the chief national and racial barriers in Europe still is its variety of languages. Several attempts have been made since the days of mediæval Latin to find a common language, but in vain. In China, however, the written charactei has supplied the many races and languages or dialects of that country with a common medium of intercommunication. Though the symbols are pronounced differently in different provinces, they are understood alike by all readers, just as the same musical score is read and played with equal ease through Europe. Consequently the common written system has been a national bond of extraordinary value, and one of the chief factors in the unity of China.

Nevertheless India did have a measure of influence which is still of considerable value in the realm of letters. During the third century A.D. a certain Chinese, Sun Yen by name, availed himself of some knowledge of Sanskrit to introduce a syllabic system for indicating the sound of a written character. By taking the initial sound of one character and the final sound of another, the sound of a third may be indicated, *e.g.* bone and dog—bog. The great imperial dictionary has the sound of all its characters indicated in this manner, a contribution of much value as a standard of correct pronunciation, and the system has value as a record of the sounds in use when it was invented. This is but one of numerous early importations into China, and it shows that, even in the conservative realm of letters, the Chinese have not been averse from the adoption of foreign ideas.

To describe in detail the variety of new ideas and knowledge introduced from India, either by Indian monks, or Chinese devout Buddhists who visited India, would be a subject to itself. On the other hand, it is well known among scholars and a remarkable fact, that for accurate knowledge of the condition of India from the fourth to the seventh centuries A.D. we are indebted to the records of Chinese Buddhist monks.

Many of them journeyed through that country, observing, recording, narrating, and their works still exist, men such as Fa Hsien (399), Sung Yun (518), Hsuan Tsang (629), I Ching (671), and others.

Another people with whom the Chinese came into early contact was the Arabs, whose name at first was Ta-zi, from Tadjiz, a name for the Persians, with whom they were confounded. These intrepid seafarers, pushing their way into the Persian Gulf, then in succeeding generations to India and Ceylon, followed the coast of the Indian Ocean to the Straits, passed up the western Pacific coast by Cochin-China and Annam to K'anp'u, or Hangchow in China. It seems probable that the Arabs reached some part of that country as early as the second century A.D. Whether they were preceded by Persians or some other race is not known. If M. Pelliot's belief is well grounded that the Chinese found their way across the Indian Ocean early in the first century A.D., they were either pioneers, which is not likely, or they followed a track already known, probably to the Arabs.

Early in the fifth century A.D., Hira on the Euphrates, seat of a dynasty of Christian kings which lasted several centuries, saw constantly moored before its dwellings ships which had come from India and China—some of them said to be of Chinese make. By the seventh century the Arabs had trading centres with permanent settlements in Canton, Ningpo, Hangchow and elsewhere on the south-east coast.

It is to the Arabs that Europe was indebted for much of its early, though very limited, knowledge of China. The accounts of Arabian travellers still have value for their description of the way there and of existing conditions. Their merchants seem to have conducted their business with the Chinese in a way profitable to both, at any rate until the new spirit of religious fanaticism engendered by Islam, when ' salvation or the sword ' both helped and hindered expansion. This spirit is seen at work in A.D. 758, when Mohammedan Arabs massacred five thousand traders and destroyed Canton with fire.

Mosques were built for their own use at their respective settlements along the coast, but it was not the seafaring Arabs who were the propagators of Islam in China. Such propagation took the line of the land route. The religion was brought by Turks from Turkestan long before that fierce race moved westward and devastated Persia, Arabia, Palestine, Egypt and Eastern Europe. It is well to bear in mind that Tartary stretched from the Caspian to the Pacific and that the Turks were one branch of the Tartar family. The eastern branch of the Tartars—the Tunghu, Tunghuses, or Hsien-pi—evolved the Koreans, Manchus and Khitans, while the western branch produced the Hsiung-nu or Huns, who were the ancestors of the Turks, Uighurs, Khirgiz and Mongols. It was Mohammedan soldiers from Turkestan who brought their religion with them into China. They came at the invitation of the Emperor Su Tung in 757 to help him in putting down a rebellion. These men settled in the country and took to themselves wives from among its people. In course of time their numbers grew, and the religion claimed a large portion of the population of Western China, as well as having numerous centres with small communities throughout the country. To-day, largely consequent on revolt and ruthless repression, it only numbers seven or eight million adherents.

Returning to the coast Arabs, we find that, after their violent outburst, in process of time trade was resumed, settlements formed and mosques rebuilt. By 877 the very large increase in foreign trade, chiefly Arab, is seen in the record of the capture by the Chinese of Canfu (K'anp'u), then near to Hangchow, where according to Abn Zaid, ' 120,000 Mohammedans, Jews, Christians, Parsees, etc.' were engaged in commerce. The figures may be seriously open to doubt, but the fact of the trade is established. The centre of Arabian trade in the Far East was at Palembang in Sumatra, and Arabian ships voyaged as far north as Shantung in China. Nor was the maritime intercommunication wholly confined to the Arabs and other foreigners, for ' Chinese vessels certainly went as far as Zanzibar.'

We may not leave this brief reference to Arabian

intercourse without mention of the world-wide revolution produced by their adoption of one of the greatest inventions of all time. Early in the Christian era the Chinese discovered the art of paper-making. This discovery is attributed to Ts'ai Lun in A.D. 105. Six hundred and fifty years later, in A.D. 751, during a fight between Arabs and Chinese, a number of the latter were taken prisoners. Among them were some who possessed the art of making paper, and they taught it to the Arabs. It took another four hundred years to reach Europe, through the Moors in Spain about the middle of the twelfth century. To-day our civilization, from books and currency notes down to newspapers, is built on this Chinese invention, and on the other invention of printing, which art they discovered in the sixth century A.D., for block printing on paper is known as early as 593. During succeeding centuries there was considerable expansion of the art, which only reached its final development when Feng Tao in the tenth century printed books in their modern form. By imperial orders the whole of the nine Confucian classics were printed as books in 932. The whole world might well give itself up to rejoicing—or mourning if preferred—in 1932, the millenium of this portentous invention. Evidence that wood engraving and the printing of pictures were in existence in the tenth century has been furnished by Sir Aurel Stein from Tun-huang. Movable type was invented between 1041 and 1049, but block printing remained in possession until a Presbyterian missionary founded the first matrices of movable type during last century.

Manichaeism seems to have reached China late in the sixth century, but it was not until 719, with the advent of a Manichaean astronomer, that it had any success. Its science had 'a great influence on Chinese astronomy,' but as a religion, though small communities were gathered in various centres, some of which continued to exist till modern times, the religion never had much hold on the Chinese. In the eighth century the Uighurs entered the Chinese capital of Lo-yang and, meeting Manichaeans there, took back with them four priests and adopted the religion. With them it rose to a certain power in Central Asia and with them it fell. The Manchu script is said to be derived through that of the Uighurs. The religion was prescribed in China in 843, after which its continued existence was illegal and precarious.

Christianity. To the Christian Occidental, perhaps one of the most interesting pages in China's foreign intercourse is that which deals with the early introduction of Christianity and its development. Nestorianism, the Syrian form of the Christian Church, found its way to China as early as 635. Our chief source of information is the now famous Nestorian Tablet erected in 781 in the capital of the Shensi province, Si-an (Hsi-an or Si-ngan), then the capital of China. From this tablet we learn that A-lo-pen (*i.e.* Rabban, or Ruben) and certain companions arrived there in **635** and were well received. One of the priests, a Persian, translated the thirty books of their scriptures into Chinese, and also helped an Indian monk to translate into Chinese a Buddhist sutra, which shows a friendly spirit.

The Chinese of those days do not seem to have had sufficient contact with Western races to make them anti-foreign, and were evidently willing to enter into relations with other peoples, however strange. Thus we find that the Emperor T'ai Tsung, 627-650, truly called the Great, welcomed to his court and made permanent provision for scholars from all nations. He received and supported Buddhists, Nestorians, Parsees, Manichaeans, and was willing to exchange wisdom with them all. Japanese, Koreans, Tibetans, Tartars, Annamese and others flocked to his court to acquire Chinese culture, thus spreading its civilization all over the Far East. So wide did his fame spread that the Caliphs Omar and Othman, and the Byzantine emperor Theodosius, sent envoys to his court. The sword of Islam drove many Zoroastrians from Persia, and they availed themselves of his remarkable hospitality. In the reign of his successor, who destroyed the raiding Japanese fleet and subdued Korea, when the Moslem Arabs invaded Persia, the Persian king sought the aid of China's governor in Kashgaria, to whom also Persian princes fled for refuge.

As to the Nestorians they flourished under the zeal of their Syrian and Persian priests.   Men high in office came under the spell of the Christian faith; for instance, one of the greatest generals of the day, a native of Shansi, became a convert. Their churches increased in number and were established in several provinces.   It seemed as if the gospel according to Nestorius would evangelize the Far East, as the Orthodox Church evangelized the north, and the Roman Church the west.   But the Nestorian priests in China, limited in number, were far removed from their base.   Islam, too, barred the way and crippled or destroyed the Syrian Church.   Moreover, in 845 a stern persecution of Buddhism occurred in China, when in addition to the suppression of a quarter of a million of Buddhist monks and nuns, two to three thousand priests of other foreign faiths, chiefly Nestorian, were also suppressed.

We find no trace of the religion again until the twelfth century, but there seems no doubt that a faithful remnant continued to exist.   During the thirteenth century, under the Mongol rule, there came a revival, whether among the Chinese Christian families, or by new importation, we do not know.   One of their number, Mark, a native of the province of Shensi, actually became Patriarch of the whole Nestorian Church, 1281-1317, under the name of Mar Jaballaha.   During the Mongol dynasty, Nestorian churches were again founded in several provinces, but they seem to have belonged to the foreign Christian officials and their followers, who accompanied the Mongol invaders from Western Asia, and there is no evidence that they ever had much influence on the Chinese themselves. With the fall of the Mongol dynasty Nestorian Christianity almost vanished, though in 1608 the Jesuit father Ricci speaks of ' the last trembling remnant of worshippers of the Cross ' as living at K'ai-feng-fu in the central province of Honan.

It may be assumed with reasonable certainty that the suppression of 845 tolled the knell of the Nestorian Chinese Church. Without the support of the Syrian priests, the Chinese Christians were no doubt crushed under the weight of surrounding superstitions, as well as despite or persecution. It is probable that they gradually drifted into Buddhism, the cult most nearly resembling their own. It may indeed be, as has been suggested, that they introduced into certain sects of Mahayana Buddhism ideas which influenced that religion, but that is a surmise as yet destitute of adequate evidence.

IV

THE MONGOLS

In the previous chapter it was shown that from the earliest times the expansion of China had acquainted its people with the aboriginal races dwelling within its present borders. As the circle was enlarged more points of contact resulted with other races, and at a period long before our era the struggle for existence had begun between the nomad and the farmer, the Hun and the Chinese, the end of it inevitably leading to the conquest of the herdsman by the ploughman. Attention was also drawn to Chinese expansion to the north-west before the Christian era. This expansion during the following millenium brought them into contact westward with Central Asia, India, Graeco-Bactria, Persia, Arabia and the Roman empire, southward with Cochin-China, the great equatorial islands, Burma and even the coast of Africa, and eastward with Korea and Japan.

The influence of this intercourse was not limited to China, for Chinese ideas were carried abroad, and the invention by the Chinese of paper and

printing during this period was destined to have
a powerful influence on the great European
renaissance.

In this chapter we shall consider the foreign
relations of China during the period from A.D. 1000
to 1500, or thereabouts. As this period is
especially notable for the terrible eruption of
another branch of the Tartars, the chapter is
entitled 'The Mongols.' Before proceeding to
that subject a few further remarks are necessary.

It is important to understand that the rise of
the Mongols was only the continuation of the
persistent southward trend of the tribes from the
prairies. The raiding horseman of the northern
plains pressed ever upon the peaceful ploughman
of the southern fields. During the early half
of the famous T'ang dynasty, A.D. 618-907, the
Chinese kept their fierce northern foes at bay.
T'ai Tsung the Great made his dynasty glorious
by his martial power, and even more by his
devotion to poetry, art, literature, and intellectual
and political development. Later, the clever
and unscrupulous Empress Wu—like the recent
Empress Dowager—set her dynasty on the way
to decline. This dynasty, famous also as the
first great period of foreign intercourse, came to
the usual ignoble end in a succession of feeble
rulers, swayed by the herd of eunuchs who have
ever infested and controlled the Chinese court.
The northern foe once more invaded the land,
and of five short-lived dynasties which arose

between 907 and 960 three were of Turcoman or Tartar origin.

One of these three was founded with the aid of the Khitans, another Tartar tribe now pressing in upon China. They are specially interesting to the West, as it is from this tribe that we derive the word ' Cathay.' The names ' Seres ' and ' China ' have already been discussed ; the third name apparently came to us through its Mongol form Kitai, which still remains the Russian name for China. Cathay then may be considered the northern name as Ts'in or China was its western name.

The Khitans first came on the scene about 480 A.D., but it was not until the tenth century that they began to play a dominant part in history. During that century they secured the hegemony of the Tartar tribes and ruled for two centuries from Korea to the Altai mountains. Between 1004 and 1125 they harried China and also conquered and held for a time a part of the north, making Peking the capital of their entire Tartar empire.

As to China itself, it was in A.D. 960 that a northern Chinese arose who overthrew the last of the five ephemeral dynasties which followed the T'ang dynasty, and, ascending the throne, founded the great Sung dynasty which lasted 320 years from 960-1280. The Sung founder and his successors had not only to keep at bay the Khitan Tartars on the north-east, but also a new

foe, the Tanguts (the Hsia, or Tibetans), on the
west. The Sung monarchs for 165 years, till
1125, maintained and developed the national
culture. In passing it may be remarked that
during this period China went through her period
of communism or nationalization. Led by the
prime minister, Wang An-Shih, an able scholar,
but as dishevelled and unwashed as the proverbial
anarchist, the country was brought into a parlous
state. It is fair, however, to say that one of the
chief objects of his communism was the development of national defence against the encroaching
northern barbarians, who unceasingly threatened
the civilization of China as the Goths threatened
that of the Roman empire.

In 1125 began the decay of the Sung rulers and
also of the Khitans. Meanwhile still another
Tartar power had arisen, known as the Kin, Chin,
or Golden Horde, and this now became the
dominant Tartar tribe. The Golden Horde broke
the power of the Khitans and drove them westward to Kashgar. Then the Horde descended
on China, seized the northern half and ruled it
for 118 years, leaving the unhappy Sung (or
Chinese) emperors only the southern half, with
the Yangtze River as the dividing line. The
decadent Sung emperors maintained their hold
upon the south for another 160 years, with their
capital at Nanking. It is noteworthy that,
despite imperial decay, and the failure of able
statesmen and gallant generals to expel the

Tartars from the north, this was one of the most brilliant literary periods in Chinese history. A greater power than that of the Sung was needed to expel the Golden Horde. This new power now arose; but it brought also the final extinction of the Sung dynasty, whose last child-sovereign perished in the waters of the Canton River in 1280.

As to Western intercourse during the Sung period, there is evidence that the sea route was maintained by the Arabs. But, with regard to the land route, the expansion of Islam formed an impassable barrier between China and Europe. During this period many Tartar tribes adopted Islam as their religion. Among these were the Uighurs, whose name in the form of Hui-ho, now Hui-hui, the Chinese adopted as the name for Islam, so that Islam in China is the 'Uighur Religion.' With the Moslem sword barring the way between Europe and Asia, and with Tartar and Tibetan hordes barring the way between China and the rest of Asia, intercommunication east and west was almost impossible. On the whole the Sung rulers had their hands too full of Tartars to take much interest in other foreign relations. If they had become anti-foreign in general—and we find no evidence that they were —there would have been ample excuse, because their age-long experience of the Tartars and even of other foreigners encouraged no love for closer intimacy, and they were soon to undergo still further discouragement.

The new force which arose, and which crushed the Golden Horde, destroyed the line of Sung, and swept with sword and flame across half the world, forms the principal subject of this chapter. The Mongols, who, to the annoyance of the Chinese, Japanese and others, have been adopted by Occidentals as their descriptive standard for the Far Eastern races, were a people as much hated by those races as they were by the people of the West.

The word Mongol means ' Brave Man.' The home of the tribe was north of the Amur River, between the Onon and Kerulon Rivers, southeast of Lake Baikal. In 1135 they began their struggle with the Golden Horde which ended in the conquest and expulsion of the latter in 1234. The Mongols took K'ai-feng-fu in Honan, which was then the northern capital of China. The Sung sovereign had sided, not unnaturally, with the new Tartar power against his old enemies the Golden Horde, in the hope of recovering China for the Chinese. His fate and that of his dynasty was to be crushed out of existence by the fierce Mongols.

If it be true that the Mongols are descendants of the Huns, then Jenghiz Khan, who welded them into the greatest, or at any rate the most widespread martial force in history, was of the same race as Attila, the ' Scourge of God,' who in the fifth century A.D. harried half of Asia and subdued most of Europe.

Jenghiz (or Genghiz, or Tchinguiz) Khan, born in 1262, whose youthful name was Temuchin, was the son of Yesugai Bahadur, whose descendants had for surname Burchukin, or ' Grey-eyed ' —which seems to hint at a non-mongoloid origin. On the death of Yesugai, the succession of the thirteen-year-old boy Temuchin was not acceptable to the Mongol tribes whom his redoubtable father had led to victory. It seemed as if there would be complete defection, as most of them gave in their adherence to Targutai, the head of another tribe. Temuchin's mother, a brave and wise woman, raised the tribal ensign and succeeded in holding the fealty of the smaller half of the tribes. In his youth Temuchin endured great hardships, was even prisoner in the hands of his rivals, and was wounded by their arrows, but, guided by his mother, he with indomitable courage succeeded in gathering an army 13,000 strong, which he hurled victoriously against 30,000 of the disloyal tribesmen. With the ferocity which marked his career, he cast his prisoners alive into eighty cauldrons of boiling water.

By the time he reached the forty-fourth year of his age, Temuchin had made his Mongols masters over the numerous tribes of Tartars inhabiting most of what we now call Mongolia, together with other adjacent tribes. At a great Kuriltai, or general assembly of Mongol chiefs, held on the banks of the Onon River, he was proclaimed Jenghiz Khan, Powerful, or Mighty

Khan. Ever restless, he year by year strengthened his position, sometimes by ruthlessly suppressing his opponents and dominating their territory, at others by arranging marriage alliances with powerful chiefs in order to increase the number of his allies, and therewith the number of the armies he could command.

He now turned his attention towards China, the northern half of which was under the Chins, or the Golden Horde. By 1213 he had overrun most of their territory, and they were glad to buy him off with promises of heavy tribute, which they in turn squeezed out of the unfortunate northern Chinese whom they ruled.

By this time he had fixed his capital at Karakoram, the old capital of the Mongol (Tartar) Confederacy. It was situated on the upper Orkhon River south-west of Urga. Thence he began to send out expeditions for the conquest of Western Asia, where with marvellous rapidity they overran Kashgar, Yarkand and Khoten, pierced the mountain passes of the Himalayas, won a great victory on the banks of the Indus, conquered Georgia in Asia Minor, and finally penetrated into Eastern Europe. The conflicting states of Russia were unable to withstand the solid impact of the Tartars, and the Czar, who had but little power over his semi-independent nobles, was compelled to come to terms with his horrible invaders by the payment of a heavy annual tribute.

Such was the ruthlessness of Jenghiz that he razed every resisting city to the ground and boasted ' that he could ride over their sites without meeting an obstacle large enough to make his horse stumble.'

As M. Cordier says : ' In their mode of action the Mongols combined pillage, cruelty, destruction without end ; all was barbarity without a noble emotion ; it was the pleasure of slaying, the love of massacre.' The Mongol avalanches that poured from their heights spread horror and destruction everywhere, without a single redeeming feature; nothing remained but the sites of levelled cities and fertile plains transformed into deserts sown with the dead bodies of tens of millions of their inhabitants. Such for at least three thousand years has marked the course of the Tartar, be he Hun, Mongol or Turk. That the civilized powers did not ages ago unite to destroy the power of these monsters can only be accounted for on the ground that they were more anxious to destroy each other—a political condition which, happily for the Turk, still continues.

With the whole of Central Asia, part of India, Persia, the Caucasus, and the east of Europe terrified and submissive, Jenghiz returned home in 1225, only to sorrow over the death of his eldest son.

In the meantime China had not been neglected. The Mongol commander, aided by the foolish and vengeful Sung emperor, attacked the Golden

Horde, who had ruled Northern China for over a century. The Golden Horde was defeated and expelled, but the Sung emperor now found himself face to face with an insatiable and implacable conqueror. Happily, the usual massacre was modified in China on the advice of the Great Khan's chief counsellor, who showed that it was better to keep the people alive to work for their conquerors than to slay them. In 1227, while the Mongol conquest of China was still in its early stages, this bloody monster, this destructive savage, Jenghiz Khan, passed away. Gifted with remarkable powers of military organization, severe in the discipline of his army, rejoicing in battle and massacre, he crushed the world as none other did before or since. Alaric, Attila, Jenghiz, Tamerlane, four Scourges of God, and of these the greatest in the extent of his conquests was Jenghiz.

Two good things resulted—accidental, not intentional—first, Islam, the other fanatical force of the world, was seriously checked; second, during the reign of his successors the land route was open for 150 years between East and West, and Europeans for the first time in history availed themselves of it. Catholic missionaries are said to have reached China by this route during the reign of Jenghiz.

After his death the immense Mongol empire was divided among his four heirs. One received the territories west and north of the Caspian, another the territory south and east of these, a third Mongolia itself, and a fourth the Far Eastern territory. The third son, Ogotai, was elected Grand Khan, and the hordes were soon again set in motion. The two western khans united their forces to subject Persia and the west as far as Bulgaria; the two eastern khans to conquer China. On the west Riazan, Moscow, Vladimir, Kieff were destroyed and their inhabitants put to the sword; the grand ducal family perishing in the burning Cathedral of Vladimir. Hungary and Poland were invaded, Pesth, Gran and Cracow being razed to the ground. In Silesia a force of 30,000 Germans, Poles and Silesians was crushed. The invaders carried away the head of the Duke Henry on the point of a lance, and filled nine great sacks with an ear from each of the slain. Moravia was given over to fire and sword as far as Bohemia and Austria, and Vienna was threatened. France and Germany were in terror of these Mongol demons, of a form and language described as inhuman. No wonder that, in 1238, even the Moslems of Asia Minor turned to their erstwhile Christian foes and implored the protection of France and of Europe against the ferocious creatures who threatened the civilized world with destruction. Happily further progress was arrested, chiefly by the news of the death of the Grand Khan, Ogotai, after a drunken debauch. His death recalled the Mongol leaders to their capital at Karakoram for the election of a new Grand Khan.

One man stands out alone from this picture of infamy. It was the Chief Counsellor of the Mongols, Ye-liu-ch'u-ts'ai. He was a Khitan, or Chin, and had been brought up at the Tartar court of the Golden Horde in China, in all the culture they gladly adopted from the Chinese, as indeed later did the Mongol conquerors. This counsellor, by his advice against slaughter, probably saved more lives, especially of Chinese, than any known personage in history.

It is noteworthy that, despite the fierceness of the Mongols when at war, they appear to have been quite approachable in times of peace. Though they terrorized Christian and Moslem alike during their raids, they had a certain admiration for the culture they destroyed, and welcomed such representatives as ventured among them. Sempad visited them as representative of the Armenian Christians. The friar Jean du Plan de Carpin, commonly styled Plan Carpin, sent by Pope Innocent IV, was actually in 1246 present, along with his companions, at the election of the new Grand Khan Kuyuk, at which also were present the Russian Duke Yaroslav, soon after poisoned there, two sons of the King of Georgia, an envoy from the Caliph of Baghdad, and so on. The new Grand Khan, Kuyuk, 1246, grandson of Jenghiz, sent back a haughty reply to the Pope by the envoys he had sent. It is of interest to learn that he had numerous Christians in his suite—probably of the Armenian Church—and that he himself ' wished to become a Christian.' There is an unsupported statement that his successor Mangku, 1251, and all his family had been baptized by an Armenian bishop. Mangku's able mother (Siurkusteni), who was also mother of his three powerful brothers Khubilai (or Kublai), Hulagu and Arik Buga, was a Christian.

William of Rubruck, a Franciscan who carried letters from St. Louis, King of France, visited Prince Khubilai's court about 1254, and his *Itinerarium* provided Roger Bacon with considerable matter for his *Opus Majus*, and Purchas much material for his *Pilgrimes*. Col. Yule ranks the *Itinerarium* as equal with the *Travels* of Marco Polo. It supplies considerable information as to the court of Khubilai Khan.

Returning to the Grand Khan Mangku we find that he resolved to subdue China. This proved to be a more difficult task than the conquest of Western Asia. During the progress of the campaign he died, apparently of dysentery.

It was with him (Mangku) that the civilization of the Mongols began. Walled towns commenced to take the place of camps, manners to be less harsh, desire for civilized intercourse with more cultured nations sprang up, embassies were encouraged, and pacific missions took the place of bloody massacres. Whether the Christian mother of Mangku and Khubilai influenced this change we do not know. Her Christianity may have been, must have been, characteristic of her period and environment ; it would be interesting to know to what extent it influenced the environment, as it generally does.

Mangku's successor, Khubilai Khan, began to reign in 1260, pursued the conquest of China, and in 1267 commenced the reconstruction of Peking on a magnificent scale, a monument to this day of his greatness. The name he gave it was Khan Balig, city of the Khan, from which we derive Cambaluc. The term Peking means Northern Capital. In order to facilitate the civilization of his people Khubilai also ordered the creation of a Mongol script, and this was the beginning of the literature, meagre though it be, of his race. Khubilai, or at any rate his followers, made the wrong choice of a religion for the development of a literature. Buddhism was adopted. It became the national religion of the Eastern Mongols, probably as a reaction from their surfeit of massacre. At any rate Buddhism had a measure of success in partly taming the savage nature of the Mongol, while also acting as an intellectual opiate. A religion which is based on a mistaken philosophy of the world, of life and of human nature, and which makes the monk, with his parasitic life, the noblest form of earthly existence, may bring more safety to the lives of the rest of humanity, certainly more than Islam, or the pagan Mongol, but its inevitable result is intellectual stupor. The fundamental force in Buddhism is escape from all earthly attachments and entry on earth into Nirvana, which in effect becomes spiritual inactivity and intellectual torpor.

It was this religion which the savage Mongol hordes of the East now adopted in its most degraded form—that of Tibetan Lamaism. Had they derived it from a Chinese source there might have been hope of progress, however small, through its connection with the more virile philosophy of the Confucian school.

The effect of higher civilization on the Mongol rulers was, while moderating their frenzy, to give them a sense of the value of civilized power. One result of this was that they opened and kept open the road between East and West, so long closed by Islam, and allowed and even encouraged intercourse. Another result was that while the thirst for more dominions was still unquenched, it was dominion, not slaughter and loot, which became the driving force. For instance, Khubilai Khan pursued the conquest of China, which he finally subjected in 1279. From the days of Jenghiz Khan sixty years were required for this success, a period longer than that which had been spent in subjecting Western Asia. But in the end, Khubilai and his successors were mastered by Chinese civilization, so solid and practical was it in comparison with that of Western Asia, disturbed, even destroyed as that culture had

been by Islam and by Mongol ferocity. Moreover, the civilization of Western Asia and Europe
was distant and lacked compactness, while that
of China was at hand, massive, impressive and
more approximately racial. At any rate it subjected Khubilai and his followers, while the
Western Mongols came under Arab and Persian
influence, became Mohammedans, and later
founded the great Mogul dynasty of India.

In the Far East Khubilai, not content with
China and his other immense possessions, sought
to bring Japan under his power. His first
immense naval expedition, like the Spanish
Armada, was destroyed by a storm and also by
the islanders. His second effected a landing but
was routed, 30,000 Mongols being slain, and
70,000 Chinese and Korean levies being reduced
to slavery. He succeeded in subjecting Annam,
Burma, Siam, the Loochoo Islands, and even
invaded Java. Thus he was Grand Khan of
almost the whole of Asia with the exception of
India and Japan. As an administrator he showed
undoubted talent. He organized the countries
he ruled, provided an admirable system of fast
couriers, in China completed that notable piece
of engineering skill, the Grand Canal, established
a celebrated astronomical observatory in Peking
—still existing—and an imperial college, and gave
peace and prosperity to China, harried for 200
years by Tartars and by civil strife.

V

MARCO POLO, THE EARLY EUROPEAN MISSIONARIES, AND THE FALL OF THE MONGOLS

IT has already been mentioned that the Mongol eruption burned a way across Asia into Central Europe. Curiosity as well as horror was stimulated in Europe, a curiosity which later began to demand satisfaction. It was not long before intrepid traders were tempted by *auri sacra fames* to risk their lives among the savages ; but not until the days of the Polo family of Venice do we have any account of these merchant venturers.

To Marco Polo we are primarily indebted for enlightenment in regard to the period of Mongol civilization. His book of travels, treated for long as mere traveller's tales, has received remarkable confirmation in our day, thanks to the services of Col. Yule and others. Columbus read it and set out westward in search of the East. When he finally reached the mainland he called it Champa, believing he had reached the coast known by that name, south of China.

The Polo family were Venetians seemingly at first, with trading posts in Constantinople and the Crimea. Nicolo, the father of Marco, and

Marco's uncle Maffeo are the first known Europeans to reach the court of Khubilai, whence
they returned with a letter and an envoy from
him to the Pope asking for a large number of
missionaries to be sent to evangelize his subjects.
The two Polo brothers arrived at Acre in April
1269 to find the Pope dead and delay in the
appointment of his successor.   The brothers soon
set out again, this time taking with them Marco,
the fifteen-year-old son of Nicolo, whose wife
had died during his absence.   They took with
them also a letter to Khubilai from the papal
legate Visconti, explaining the delay in acceding
to his request for missionaries.   Visconti was
soon afterwards elected Pope—Gregory X—and
sent to accompany the Polos two Dominicans.
These soon were terrified of the way and returned
to Europe.   The date of the Polos' departure
was probably in November 1271, and after
traversing Asia by land, crossing the Pamirs and
passing through Kashgar, they reached the court
of the Grand Khan in May 1275.   Think of it,
three years and a half on the way to Peking!
We make the journey now, travelling double
the distance, in two weeks.

Khubilai welcomed the travellers, and was
specially interested in the youth Marco because
of his good humour, his powers as a raconteur
and his intelligence.   He employed him on many
missions to distant parts of China, the first
between 1277-80 to Shansi, Shensi, Szechwan

and Yunnan. In telling of the last-named province he describes the war with Burma, in which,
despite their use of elephants, at first a terror to
the Mongols, the Burmese were beaten. For
three years also Marco was ruler over Yang-chou,
an important city and county on the River
Yangtze. This is the only case recorded in
history of a European being made by the emperor
' mandarin ' over Chinese territory.

After twenty years of residence in China, the
elder Polos at any rate grew homesick, nor had
twenty years of service even under the Grand
Khan dulled the natural desire of Marco to
return to his beautiful Venice. In vain did they
hint their desire to the Grand Khan, for he turned
a deaf ear. Finally a happy chance occurred, of
which they promptly availed themselves. It
happened that the Mongol Khan of Persia lost
his wife in 1286. Before she died he promised
her that he would seek her successor from the
family of the Grand Khan Khubilai. In response
the latter selected a princess, seventeen years of
age, and entrusted her to the three envoys from
Persia to convey her by sea to her destination.
The Polos, by this time no doubt well versed in
Oriental methods, found means of inspiring the
envoys with a sense of their own value for so
perilous a voyage. In consequence, the envoys
made such representations to the Grand Khan
for the experienced aid of these famous travellers,
that he reluctantly gave his consent, stipulating

that they should return to his court after their
journey. They accordingly set out early in
1292, to add the perils of the sea route to those of
the land route so long ago experienced. Anyone
who looks at a large scale map thoughtfully will
be filled with astonishment at the feat performed
by these remarkable men.

Harassed by bad weather they were detained
a long time in Sumatra. In due course they
proceeded and passed south of India. Two of
the envoys died on the way. The surviving
envoy, the Polos and the young princess reached
Persia, only to find the Khan Arghun had died
nearly a year before her departure from China.
His brother Kaikhatu reigned in his stead.
Kokachin, the princess, married Ghazan the son
of her intended husband Arghun. Arghun had
been counted one of the handsomest men of his
day, while his son Ghazan made up for ordinary
appearance by extraordinary intelligence. The
princess parted from the companions of her three
years' voyage with sorrow, and they went on their
way via Tabriz and Constantinople, arriving in
Venice in 1295. One cannot but admire the
fortitude of this maiden of seventeen, who can
never have seen the sea till she set out on her
long voyage. It was an adventure into the vast
unknown—like sailing into eternity. Was her
value of life low ?—or is our value of adventure
high ? And these men, who for the sake of gain,
or adventure, or both, counted not their lives

dear to them! They gave nothing to the Western world with intent—they gave much by accident. For it was largely through Marco Polo's account, fabulous though it seemed, that Europe began to take an interest in China.

The Polos convinced their relatives of their *bona fides* by the display of their wealth—they had not come to ask aid but to give it! Such tales did Marco tell of the millions of China that he became known as Messer Millione. Soon afterwards the Genoese, jealous of the rising mercantile powers of Venice, resolved to resist and reduce it. Marco was one of the first to offer to fit out and command a ship against the Genoese. On September 7, 1298, the Venetians were terribly defeated, Marco was captured, and for over a year remained a captive in Genoa. Among his fellow prisoners was a man of Pisa, named Rusticien, to whom he dictated in French the account of his travels—an account which was destined to have a greater influence on Europe than that of any other traveller since his day. Released in 1299 he returned to Venice, married, and died about 1325.

Somewhat late in the day the Church, in half-hearted fashion, more seriously undertook to send the light of the Gospel to the savage destroyers of humanity.

The Franciscan John of Plano Carpini had already been sent by Pope Innocent in 1245. He and his companions reached the Mongol capital

Karakoram, S.W. of Urga and the old seat of the Mongols. The mission never saw China proper, for it was only sent to the Mongol court, and was apparently diplomatic rather than propagandist. At any rate he returned after two and a half years' absence, bringing as already stated, from Kuyuk, the Grand Khan, a haughty answer to the Pope's letter.

It was another Franciscan, John of Monte Corvino, who became the apostle to the Mongols, as had been the Nestorians to the Chinese six centuries before. We have already seen that the Grand Khan Khubilai sent a message by the two elder Polos to the Pope, asking for missionaries to teach his people. That message was delivered in 1269 to one who soon afterwards became Pope Gregory X. What effect, if any, this communication had on his successor Nicholas IV we do not know, but exactly twenty years later, in 1289, Nicholas sent John of Monte Corvino with letters to all the leading khans and authorities on his way to Peking, and especially to the Grand Khan Khubilai. On the way, in India, he lost his sole companion and arrived alone in Khanbalik (Peking) apparently in 1292 or 1293. This was a year or so after the Polos left, and not long before the death of Khubilai in 1294. Corvino tells in a letter that he presented his credentials in person to Khubilai, who welcomed him and granted him a regular and seemingly liberal allowance. Quite clearly he had complete liberty to evangelize at will, that is, except for opposition he met from certain Nestorian Christians—Syrians, not Chinese. He was also embarrassed by a Lombardy doctor who had arrived two years before him, and had spoken every ill against the papal court, the Franciscans and the state of Europe in general. Corvino was nine years alone before Friar Arnold of Cologne joined him. Despite Nestorian jealousy he succeeded in establishing a mission, which prospered greatly among the variety of peoples who were present at the court of the Grand Khan in Peking, especially among the Mongols. So encouraging was his success that in 1307 the Pope sent him seven colleagues, each created ' bishop,' with authority to consecrate John as Archbishop of Cambaluc. The perils of the journey may be clearly seen in the fact that of these seven, three died on the way to India, and a fourth gave up the journey in order to return home. Thus three only reached their destination. When Corvino died about 1328, some eighty years of age, there were said to be 100,000 Catholic converts.

That there were other Europeans in Peking is clear from their mention in Corvino's letters. One of them was Pierre de Lucalongo, a Christian merchant. Amongst other places a mission of some importance was established on the south-eastern coast at Zaitun, *i.e.* Ch'uang-chow in Fukien, no doubt more in the interests of

foreigners and the Mongol garrison than of the
Chinese. Corvino had but three successors as
archbishops. The last of them was Jacques de
Florence, who along with another priest was
'martyred' in 1362, no doubt by the Chinese,
during the fall of the hated Mongol dynasty, with
which the Christian priests were so closely
associated.

Before passing to other visitors to China,
mention may be made of ' Prester John,' a name
which was well known in Europe at that period.
Crusaders in the twelfth century reported that
a Christian prince, a Nestorian, in Central Asia
was rendering aid to the Christian West against
the Moslems. Marco Polo mentions him under
the name of George, or Aung Khan, and says
that he was an ally of Jenghiz Khan. In reality
Prester John and his Christian people were the
Tartar Ongut tribe of Kansu in China, the first
of whose Christian chiefs seem to have been
Särgis (George) and his son Johanan or John.
He was a petty chief, whose power and influence
were of a modest character.

Odoric of Pordenone set off from Padua to
China in 1318, with an Irish friar as companion.
Of the two main routes he chose that by sea. It
was much longer but far less hazardous than
the land route taken by the Polos. Moreover,
Christian communities were already established
at various ports on the way. The Mameluke
Sultan of Egypt had made travel via Suez so

oppressive and risky to merchants and pilgrims alike, that they found the Mongol of Persia by comparison a friend. Odoric therefore travelled by way of Constantinople, the Black Sea, Trebizond, Erzeroum and through Persia. This route had seriously crippled the trade through Baghdad, and with it the important trade of the Venetians, Genoese and Spaniards. It will be seen, therefore, that the older trade route was changed through the oppression of the Sultan of Egypt, 1310-1341, and also through the encouragement to trade given by the Mongol rulers. Moreover, a distinct advantage was offered by the Persian land route to Constantinople, in shortening the exposure of delicate spices to the influence of the sea.

Odoric travelled by land to Ormuzd and thence by sea to Tannah (near Bombay) in India, where he lodged with a Nestorian, whom his theology compelled him to contemn. Wherever he travelled in the East he found Christianity only under the form condemned by his Church—that of Nestorianism. He travelled along the coast of Malabar, calling at various places, visited the reputed tomb of St. Thomas, proceeded across to Ceylon, thence eastward over the Indian Ocean to Sumatra, later to Java, northward to Borneo touching at Banjarmasin, whence he reached Cambodia (Champa), followed the Cochin-China coast to China, where he made Canton. Thence he followed the China coast, visiting various ports,

including Zaitun (Ch'uang-chow), and Quinsay
(Hangchow).   From there he proceeded to Nanking and Yangchow, and travelled by the new
Grand Canal to Cambaluc or Peking, where he
stayed with John of Monte Corvino for three
years.   In his valuable records he describes the
court and many other features of the country.
In due course he returned to Europe by way of
Shansi, Shensi, Szechwan and perhaps Tibet,
where it is said he was the first European visitor
to Lhassa.   Altogether he was absent from home
twelve years, three only of which were spent in
Peking.   On his return, after dictating his records, he set out to visit the Pope at Avignon, in
order to urge the immediate despatch of fifty
missionaries to the Far East ; but on the way
St. Francis of Assisi appeared to him, and told
him to return to Padua, where he would die in
ten days.   He returned and died, 1331, when only
forty-five years of age.   His records provide a
fund of material showing the relations of the
West and the East in the fourteenth century.

In 1338 an embassage purporting to come from
the Grand Khan of Cathay was received by the
Pope.   Included in it were representatives of
the Alains, a Christian tribe of Tartars.   Their
power at one time extended as far south as the
source of the Ganges.   After their departure the
Pope sent four legates to Peking.   They left in
December 1338, reached Peking in the summer of
1342, and stayed there three or four years.   They

took with them a special present of European horses, one of which was of such height and quality that it evoked general admiration. John of Marignolli, one of the four legates, has left an account of his land journey and his return by sea.

During the same period a Franciscan mission was making rapid headway in Central Asia ; but about 1340 the massacre of the ruling family by a usurper resulted in the destruction of both priests and converts.

It may be added that twenty-six monks and six lay brothers arrived in Peking to strengthen the mission of John of Monte Corvino. One of these, Nicholas, became his successor in 1333. In all fourteen archbishops of Peking were consecrated, but only three of them ever resided there. The last of the fourteen, Alexandre de Caffa, was taken prisoner by the Turks in 1475, spent seven years in captivity, and died in Italy in 1483. Some tens of missionaries reached China, but they entirely disappeared with the overthrow by the Chinese of the Mongol dynasty. This took place in 1368, though strife continued for some years afterwards.

It was a Chinese, who rose from deep poverty, that broke the power of the decadent descendants of Khubilai Khan. His family had died of famine fever. Left alone, a youth, he entered a Buddhist monastery. Later he doffed the cassock and donned the casque to expel the hated Mongols. Succeeding in this tremendous enterprise he became Emperor of China and founder of the great Ming dynasty. This was in A.D. 1868.

For nearly two centuries foreign relations between China and the West seem to have lapsed. At this we need not be surprised. Islam was a black blot on the map between Europe and Asia ; Moslem powers barred the sea route and Tartars the land route.

The Ming dynasty at first was not opposed to external relations. During the fourteenth and fifteenth centuries they opened communications with Nepal and Burma and even with the terrible Mongol Tamerlane of Samarcand. About 1400 the Ming emperor, Yung-lo, sent three envoys, one to Java and Sumatra, one to Siam and a third to Bengal. In 1405 he sent an able eunuch, Ch'eng Ho, with a fleet of 62 ships carrying 37,000 men, together with presents of silk and gold to Cochin-China, Sumatra, Java, Cambodia, Siam and other places. In 1408, the same envoy reached Ceylon. These expeditions may have been meant to reveal the might of China, for all these countries undertook to pay ' tribute.' Later Malacca and other states were brought into similar relations. Aden seems to have been the most western point the envoy reached—in 1422. A similar expedition, as far as Aden, was sent in 1431. These were the last expeditions sent West by the Chinese, for the Mongols again occupied the attention of the Ming sovereigns and the usual dynastic decay also began to appear.

The Japanese ravaged the Chinese coast for the first time in 1368. This was in the north. Later they repeated their raids in 1374 and 1387 on the south, showing special affection for the rich provinces of Kiangsu and Chekiang. These Japanese raids and those which followed influenced China's future attitude even towards intercourse with Occidentals. A distrust of all foreigners was aroused. Nor was such distrust unreasonable seeing that China had but recently shaken off the yoke of the Mongol, against whose race her people had struggled all through the ages of history.

As already stated, after the expulsion of the Mongols and their European associates, the land route was closed and so remained for two centuries. That the Chinese were on guard against the Tartars was only part of the reason for this closure. A far more serious barrier had been raised in the west of Asia by the rise of the Seljuks, and their victorious march towards the West. These Turks in their turn were fated to meet with the last of the Mongol destroyers. It was a descendant of Jenghiz Khan, Tamerlane (or Timur) of Samarcand, who in the plains of Angora arrested the march of the Seljuks and thereby, though not with that intent, retarded for half a century the fall of Constantinople into the hands of the Ottoman Turks. Tamerlane not only curbed the Turks, but also swept into India as far as Delhi. From Delhi to Syria, from

Persia to the borders of China he piled up mountains of skulls and razed to the ground imposing
cities. In 1405 early death alone stopped him
from easily carrying out his intention to recover
China for his race. A century later, in 1526, his
descendant Baber founded the great Mogul empire
in India.

As to the sea route, the names only of three
Europeans who visited the seas of Asia during
this period are left to us, for the Moslems ruled
Northern Africa, straddled across the Red Sea
and the Persian Gulf, and for a time held the chief
ports of Asia. Undoubtedly the main barrier to
European intercourse with the East was Moslem
control of the Red Sea and the Persian Gulf, and
this will be again referred to in the next chapter
on ' The Opening of the Sea Route.' We know
that this was the prime cause of the European
search for a sea passage, in order to avoid Moslem
territory. That search resulted in the discovery
of America and the doubling of the Cape of Good
Hope by Vasco da Gama. It must also be
remembered that in the fourteenth and fifteenth
century conditions in Europe were the worst
possible for trade expansion, for the Christian
warrior was so busy slaying his fellow Christians
and devastating their lands, that he had no
time to defend Christendom against the Moslem
intruder.

As to the Chinese, however chary they may
have been of opening their northern frontier,

the early Ming rulers were ready enough for external relations by sea, especially if these relations should make China glorious in Asia. Mention has already been made of the expeditions sent out by the Ming emperors which reached the Persian Gulf. It is worthy of note that these are the only attempts ever made by the Chinese to become a great sea power and the suzerain of Asia. It may not be impossible for that attempt to be repeated, unless humanity learns to spend its energy in making itself more beautiful in a world of beauty, rather than in fertilizing its furrows and dyeing its seas with human blood.

VI

THE OPENING OF THE SEA ROUTE AND THE ADVENT OF THE ENGLISH

THE last decade of the fifteenth century is well known to be one of the most important in the history of East and West.

In 1492 Columbus set out to reach China, and on his third voyage, in 1496, thought he had made Champa to the south of that country. In 1497 John Cabot, also searching for China, discovered North America. In 1498 the Portuguese Vasco da Gama, seeking India and China, actually found his way to the Indies after doubling the Cape of Good Hope.

As shown in the last chapter it was the Moslem powers that barred the way to the Far East. Western India, Central Asia, Persia, Arabia, Asia Minor, Syria, Egypt, North Africa were in their hands—lands scorched with the flame of their fanaticism. Spain itself had been for centuries under Moslem dominance, with consequent reaction on the character of its people, for they developed a similar religious fanaticism at home and abroad. It was only in 1492 that they threw off the Moslem yoke.

62

This formidable barrier, stimulating as it did the ardent desire of the Western world to find again a way to the Orient, caused Columbus, Cabot, da Gama to set out on their daring quest. In 1520 it sent Magellan round the south of America to meet his death during a fight in the Philippines. It was the lure of China that sent Sebastian Cabot and Sir Hugh Willoughby in 1553 in search of the north-west passage, carrying letters from Edward the Sixth to ' kings, princes and other potentates inhabiting the north-east parts of the world in the direction of the powerful empire of Cathay.' It sent Richard Chancellor to discover the White Sea in 1554, whence, finding he was not in China but in Russia, he proceeded to Moscow and obtained the first licence to trade with that country, via the Dvina. Jenkinson followed him in 1557, still aiming at Cathay, and penetrated as far inland as Bokhara via Russia in December 1558.

Through Sir Humphrey Gilbert, Frobisher was authorized in 1575 to renew the search for the north-west passage under the ' Cathay Company.' In 1580 Jackman and Pet set out to seek the north-west passage, their aim being to make for Cathay, pass the winter in Marco Polo's Quinsay (Hangchow) and then proceed to Japan, where they were correctly told they would find Christians. The expedition of course failed. Other attempts to find the north-west passage were made in 1602 by George Waymouth, in 1607 by

Henry Hudson who later found Hudson's Bay, in 1612 by Sir Thomas Button, and in 1612-19 by William Baffin of Baffin's Bay renown. The aim of all these attempts to discover the north-west passage was China. The world had been proved to be round, and though the coast of America was as yet scarcely known, sufficient knowledge had been acquired to justify the belief that beyond America lay China.

In 1573 William Bourne published his work, *A Regiment of the Sea*, in which he showed that five routes to China were possible : the Portuguese route by the Cape of Good Hope ; the Magellan Straits route ; the north-west route ; the north-east and north of Russia route ; and the northern route (presumably via the Pole). In 1577-80 Drake circumnavigated the globe. In passing, it may be noted that the first English missionary to reach India was the Jesuit, Thomas Stephens of New College, Oxford, who arrived at Goa in 1579 and died there in 1619. Thomas Cavendish was the second Englishman to circumnavigate the globe in 1586-8. He captured the *Santa Anna*, from which he received a valuable prize in the shape of a chart of China.

In 1592 Sir John Burrough, in connection with Sir Walter Raleigh's expedition against the Spaniards, captured the *Madre de Dios*, of 1600 tons. This immense ship, the wonder of the English, gave up to them their first authentic detail of the secret of the commerce of the Far

East, which they had vainly sought for long to surprise!

Four years later, in 1596, at the expense chiefly of Sir Robert Dudley, Benjamin Wood set out with three ships and a letter in Latin from Queen Elizabeth to the Emperor of China. She assured the Emperor of the good faith of the traders, Richard Allen (or Allott) and Thomas Bromfield, who had equipped the vessels with merchandise, and recommended them to His Majesty's protection. At the same time she begged him to inform her through them of the measures by which the empire of China had become so celebrated for its commerce. She also offered protection to Chinese subjects in any of her ports they might visit. There is little further news concerning this unfortunate expedition. The ships took the westward route, captured two or three Portuguese ships, but officers and men were carried off by illness, and all save four sailors are believed to have perished. These four, when nearing Porto Rico, were met by a Spanish pirate, who in the pitiless spirit of the period slew two, and poisoned a third, only one escaping alive.

In 1600 the Merchant Venturers of London sent out five ships under James Lancaster, who returned in 1603, having succeeded in establishing a station at Bantam in Java. In the same year the London East India Company, known as ' The Old Company,' was formed under the title ' The

Governour and Company of Merchants of London trading into the East Indies,' which existed till 1708 when it was absorbed by ' The United Company of Merchants of England trading to the East.'

The Old Company in 1604 sent out four ships under Henry Middleton which sailed as far as the Moluccas.   In the same year Sir Edward Michelborne set off on an independent expedition ' to discover the countries of Cathay, China, Japan, Corea and Cambodia and the islands and countries adjacent, and to trade with the inhabitants.' The celebrated John Davis of Arctic fame, one of Michelborne's captains, was killed in a fight with the Japanese, and the conduct of Michelborne has been described as piratical and injurious to the interests of traders.   He returned in 1606.

Another search was organized for the northwest passage in 1606, when John Knight set sail ; but he died off the coast of Labrador, and the *Hopewell* returned.   The Keeling expedition, 1606-9, reached Java and established a ' factory.' Four other expeditions followed, for the most part unsuccessfully.

Consequent on services rendered by William Adams, who had reached Japan on a Dutch ship, in organizing the navy of Japan, 1600-1620, John Saris found a welcome in that country when he carried letters from James I to its court.   Iyeyasu, father of the Shogun, in 1613 authorized the opening of ports to the British. Factories were established in four centres, but trading expeditions from there to Cochin-China and Siam were unfortunate. The Dutch also were serious rivals, and a new Shogun opposed to foreigners soon limited trade to Hirado (near Nagasaki). The English closed their factory in 1623; and in 1624, through hatred of the Catholics, a decree was issued expelling all foreigners from Japan.

Attention has been drawn to these early relations with Japan, because that country was considered as a ' jumping-off ' place to China, and several unsuccessful plans were made to that end. Moreover, it is from Japan that we first hear of tea, which is mentioned by its ordinary Chinese name ' cha ' in 1615. Not until 1660, in Pepys's *Diary*, do we find it mentioned in its Southern Chinese form of ' tay ' or tea.

The first English ship actually to reach China did so too impetuously, the *Unicorn* from Java to Japan being wrecked on its coast near Macao in 1620. The natives treated the crew civilly and sold them two boats, one of which was soon captured by the Portuguese ; the other reached its destination.

The whole situation was one of international jealousy, intrigue, hatred, strife. Portuguese against Dutch, Spaniards against British, each against the other, or on his side as international disputes or immediate advantage served. For instance, a prophecy was arranged for the Emperor of China that a people with grey eyes would subdue his nation ; this instilled hatred into the Chinese against the British—whom as a matter of fact they had never seen. Not that there seems to have been much to choose between all these fearless adventurers, hard of hand and heart, ready to trade or raid as might seem the more profitable.

Henry Bornford is considered to have been, in 1636, the first Englishman to trade with China, though even then he did not do so direct, but through Macao, and in the interests equally of the Portuguese, whom at that time the Dutch were blockading. John Weddell was the first Englishman to open up communication direct with China. Sir William Courteenes in 1635, despite the opposition of the Old Company, obtained a licence from Charles I to attempt to open up commerce with China and Japan, and John Weddell commanded the flotilla of six ships which sailed from The Downs, 14th April, 1636. He reached Macao, and despite Portuguese opposition, proceeded to Canton. The Chinese, influenced by the Portuguese, refused to trade and attacked him. In self defence he seized a small native fort, but as his supercargoes ashore were imprisoned by the Chinese, he had to seek the aid of the Portuguese to obtain their release, and sailed away in December 1637.

Another fleet was sent out by the Old Company

in June 1637, which carried a letter from Charles I to the Portuguese Governor of Macao. That governor informed the bearers that the Chinese had caused the Portuguese to suffer severely in consequence of the misconduct of Weddell the previous year; news which the rival Company would not be grieved to hear!

It may here be said that Peter Mundy, a merchant who accompanied Weddell's expedition, left a valuable account of his observations. The MSS. is in the Bodleian and is being published by the Hakluyt Society.

In 1643 the *Hind* reached Macao; but trade was at a standstill consequent on the fall of the great Ming dynasty and the advent of the Tartar, or Manchu, ruler. In 1658 the *King Ferdinand* and the *Richard and Martha* found Canton. Their supercargoes also found the demands of the officials so oppressive that they lifted their anchors in surreptitious flight. The frigate *Surat* arrived at Macao in 1664; but such were the demands of the Portuguese, who also refused to permit a 'factory' to be established there, that the *Surat* sailed away to Java. In 1671 the English established a 'factory' on the mainland in Amoy, which was then under Koxinga, who had driven the Dutch out of the island of Formosa (ceded in 1894 to the Japanese); but Koxinga being soon afterwards driven out of Amoy by the new Manchu power, the English also had to depart. Other ships were sent by the

English, but the Portuguese maintained their monopoly and their men-of-war sought to capture the English trading vessels. The Old Company succeeded in establishing a temporary factory in Canton in 1684. In 1689 the *Defence* reached Canton, but oppressive demands and a brawl in which its doctor, some of its sailors and a Chinese were killed, caused that effort likewise to fail.

The Honourable East India Company was formed in 1708-9, and Allen Catchpoole was appointed its representative in China, as also he was made envoy of the King of England. His instructions were to negotiate for a settlement in Ningpo (Liampo) or at Nanking, or elsewhere. He arrived at Chusan Island off Ningpo, where Gough had already begun to construct a ' factory.' The English were expelled in 1702, and Catchpoole was murdered in 1705 at Pulo Condor.

The year 1699 is that in which British commerce really began at Canton. For 200 years the British had sought China, or, having found it, struggled vainly to obtain a foothold. The *Macclesfield* was the first ship to trade there peaceably. After the formation of the great East India Company in 1708-9, other British ships reached the coast, the *Anne* in 1713, the *Bonitta* and the *Cadogan* in 1721, the *Walpole* in 1723, and other boats in the interim. Such were the local extortions in Canton, that the *Normanton* in 1736 sought, though in vain, to establish a settlement at Ningpo, as had been previously attempted at Amoy and on the Chusan Island. Representations were somehow made to Peking, and on the accession of the Emperor Ch'ien Lung in 1736 orders were issued which, by forbidding extortion, acknowledged the trade.

In 1741 Commodore Anson arrived at Canton in the *Centurion* ; in 1742 Capt. Congreve in the *Onslow.* Harrison and Flint, the latter twenty-five years in the country, visited Ningpo, but were ordered not to return there. In 1757 an imperial edict confined all trade, save the Russian, to Canton. Flint, one of the first Englishmen to learn Chinese, set off for the north with a petition to the Throne against the oppressive conditions of trade. He only reached Tientsin, but his petition was forwarded. The Emperor ordered an enquiry, consequent on which the local Superintendent of Trade (Hoppo) was dismissed ; but the Governor had the English merchants beaten by his soldiers in his Yamen ; Flint was deported ; and the Chinese scholar who had dared to write out Flint's memorial to the Throne was beheaded. For a time, by imperial orders, conditions were improved, but local oppression soon increased ; none might teach a foreigner the Chinese language on pain of death ; Englishmen were executed without proof of crime ; justice was a mockery. Something had to be done, for the position of traders in the only dwelling-place permitted to them, a miserable suburb of Canton, was intolerable. The British Government determined to send an ambassador to Peking. Colonel Cathcart was appointed and set out from England. His vessel, the *Vestal*, was lost in 1788 in the Straits of Sunda. In 1792 Lord Macartney was appointed in his place, and with him travelled Sir G. L. Staunton as secretary. Staunton's son, George Thomas, accompanied his father. He was then a boy of fifteen, later became learned in the Chinese language and literature, and was one of the founders of the Royal Asiatic Society. John Barrow acted as private secretary to Lord Macartney and published an account of the voyage. The ambassador and his suite set out in the *Lion*, the *Hindustan*, and the *Jackal* on 16th Sept., 1792. The question of an interpreter was a serious one. Flint, the only Englishman who knew any Chinese, was forbidden the country. The interpreter Galbert, lent by the French to Colonel Cathcart, had gone down with the *Vestal*. The Lazarists and the ' Missions Étrangères ' justifiably declined to assist. Two young Chinese were found in a theological college at Naples, who agreed to serve as interpreters ; but they were of a class that knew nothing of court or diplomatic etiquette and ' their inexperience was not one of the least causes of the non-success of the mission.' The ships called at Formosa, the Chusan Islands, and reached Tientsin, whence Lord Macartney and his suite proceeded to

Peking, arriving there the 21st Aug., 1793.   The
aim of the embassage was to obtain permission
for traders to settle at Ningpo, in the Chusan
Islands, at Tientsin and, like the Russians, to have
a depot in Peking ;   also to secure the proper
regulation of trade under the strict application
of the imperial tariff.

The Emperor had gone to Jehol, his summer
residence beyond the Great Wall, where Macartney toilfully followed him.   Ch'ien Lung, a great
emperor, treated him with courtesy, but replied
to the letter of George III refusing all his requests.
The fact is, as P. de Grammont indicates, the
envoy and his staff were totally ignorant of the
normal methods of approach.   They carried no
presents ;   they failed to do obeisance (kotow),
without explaining the reason ;   their dress was
unimposing ;   they ' buttered no paws ' ;   and
had neither style nor tone to impress the court.
Moreover, de Grammont adds, ' Another reason
for their ill success, and to me the principal one,
was the intrigues of a certain missionary (a
Portuguese, Joseph-Bernard de Almeida), who,
imagining that the embassage would injure the
trade of his country, did not fail, in consequence,
to sow well notions unfavourable to the English.'
So it came to pass that the ambassador of the
King of Great Britain was looked upon as a mere
' bearer of tribute,' a title indeed inscribed on the
flags flown on his barges, which were supplied by
Chinese.   He returned by way of the Grand

Canal, Hangchow, and Canton, leaving China 17th March, 1794.   The voyage had cost £80,000 and was fruitless—all through ignorance on both sides.

Such then was the position of the British at the close of the eighteenth century.

VII

CHINESE EXPANSION AND THE ADVENT OF OTHER NATIONS

LET us now consider the attempts made by the Chinese rulers for external expansion during this period. First, we may briefly refer to the foreign affairs of the Ming dynasty, 1368-1644. At the outset this dynasty had a prolonged struggle with the expelled Mongols, a struggle often renewed. Nevertheless, communication was opened with Tamerlane in Western Asia, who assumed friendship, but whose timely death undoubtedly saved China from a further Mongol subjugation. It has already been shown that in the fifteenth century the Ming Emperor despatched envoys to Java, Sumatra, Siam and Bengal. The expedition of the eunuch Ch'eng Ho followed. In 1405 he set off with 62 ships, 37,000 men, and presents of silk and gold. With these he visited Cochin-China, Sumatra, Java, Cambodia, Siam. The states which refused to accept gifts and return tribute were attacked and subdued. In 1408 Ch'eng Ho sailed again, reached Ceylon and carried off the ' king ' and his family, who had attempted to imprison the Chinese envoy. A tablet exists at Galle inscribed in Chinese, Tamil and Persian, mentioning a second visit of Ch'eng Ho in 1409.   For fifty years Ceylon paid tribute to China.   In 1416 Malacca, Calicut and seventeen other southern and western countries—one of them Bengal—sent envoys with ‘ tribute.’   In 1430 Ch'eng Ho sailed as far as Ormuzd.   Further expeditions were made in the middle of the fifteenth century, but these were the last of any importance made by the Chinese Government. With the advent of the Ch'ing, or Manchu, dynasty, steady expansion from within took the place of these external adventures.

Japan we need not discuss, save to say that during the 300 years now under review its sea-faring folk traded and raided along the coast of China as opportunity served.   The south-eastern coast was so much at their mercy, that at one time the Emperor of China ordered all towns and villages to be withdrawn ten miles from the shore. They appeared for the first time in 1369.   From 1546 to 1570 there are a dozen records of their attacks on various parts of the seaboard and even of their seizing important inland towns.   Their incursions into Korea, of which China was suzerain, were constant.   The famous Japanese, Hideyoshi, ambitious to conquer China, sought an alliance for that purpose with the Koreans. Their refusal resulted in a prolonged war, which began in 1592 and lasted till 1607, China rendering constant aid to the Koreans.

It was during the latter half of the Ming dynasty, *i.e.* during the sixteenth century, that the Chinese began to close their country to the foreigner. Nor need we be surprised. To an age-long history of Tartar aggression on the north and west was now added the anxiety of a huge coast line, at the mercy of a piratical nation like the Japanese, and of a new influx of men of barbarous breed, with a language that no civilized tongue could utter'; beards black, brown, and even red ; eyes not a decent black or brown, but like those of cats, blue and grey ; and of a manner ferocious. It was high time that China shut itself in to itself, and excluded foreign wares which it did not need. The Ming policy of exclusion, or at any rate restriction, was inherited by the succeeding dynasty of the Tartar Manchus, who, with Chinese aid, overthrew that of the Ming in 1644. The Manchus maintained the same policy, with increased rigour, until the unhappy arbitration of the gun was invoked.

Portugal. It is to Portugal that we owe the reopening of the sea route between East and West. The barrier of Islam, impregnable to a frontal attack, had to be turned. The Portuguese were the people who made the first venture and succeeded. Unknown as a seafaring race they began, under Henry the Navigator, to create navies and sailors, and for nearly a hundred years —during the whole of the fifteenth century—they slowly crept farther and farther down the west

coast of Africa, which tradition said was surrounded by water, feeling their way to the East.
The spices of the Indies, the silks of China, the
Central Asian Christian ruler Prester John—
these were the perennial attraction. At last
Vasco da Gama set sail from Lisbon on Sunday,
8th July, 1497, in the *St. Gabriel*, accompanied
by three other ships. By 22nd November he
had doubled the Cape of Good Hope, and on the
25th December gave its name to Natal, where he
spent Christmas. On the 20th May, 1498, he
cast anchor in Calicut, and arrived back in
Lisbon, September 1499.

One bows in admiration before these gallant
adventurers, while deploring the excesses into
which some of them were led. Moslems and
Tartars have been and are the desert makers of
the world. It was Moslem power in the Indian
Ocean that Vasco da Gama, Francisco de Almeida,
Tristan da Cunha and Alfonso de Albuquerque
had to face. It opposed them everywhere, for
Islam held the strategic points and the marts
across the world, from Morocco on the Atlantic
to Java in the Pacific. Da Gama, attacked by
the Moslems, replied with energy. Almeida broke
the Moslem sea power. Albuquerque made the
Portuguese masters of the East by holding Ormuz,
Goa and Malacca, which last port is described by
Lodovico de Varthemna as then the premier port
of the world.

It was at Malacca that the Portuguese came

into contact with junks trading between China and the Malay archipelago. The Chinese traders had no love for the Moslem rulers in Malacca, who overawed the native populations and oppressed the traders. By warning de Sequeira, who became the founder of Portuguese trade there, they saved him from death by poison, and his ship from destruction, though a number of Portuguese were thrown into prison. The King of Portugal had stated detailed questions for de Sequeira to answer in regard to China, which was the ultimate object of interest to Portugal. When Albuquerque arrived, 1st July, 1511, to avenge the attempt on de Sequeira, to release the Portuguese prisoners and to seize Malacca as his *point d'appui* furthest east, the Chinese trading fleet immediately offered him its services, and, after his victory, congratulated him on his success. Two brothers distinguished themselves in the stern encounter, who became, one famous, the other infamous, in connection with China; their names were Ferdinand and Simon de Andrade.

The Portuguese Alvarez was the first European to reach China by sea, but he only made Port Namoa, on an island south of Canton. That was in 1514. Rafael Perestrello, a relative of Columbus, is the first European known to have landed on the mainland from the sea. He reached China in a Malay junk with thirty Portuguese followers in 1516. After some difficulties he was

successful with the Chinese and returned to
Malacca. All honour to the Spaniards and Portu-
guese of that wonderful period, Columbus and
America in 1492, da Gama and Africa and India
in 1498, Albuquerque and Malacca in 1511, and
Perestrello and China in 1516 !

In 1517 Ferdinand Andrade with four Portuguese and four Malay ships carried to China
cargoes of pepper—symbolic of coming irritation !
Ferdinand's 'amiability, honesty and justice'
won the favour of the Chinese. He had brought
with him an envoy, Tomé Pirez, carrying letters
from the Portuguese King to the Emperor. All
seeming favourable for the mission, and having
arranged for Pirez and his staff to proceed
overland to Peking, Ferdinand Andrade set sail
to report at Malacca. His success excited the
Portuguese; and Ferdinand's brother Simon,
having obtained authority from the Governor of
India, set sail with three junks and reached the
coast of China in 1519. Simon, of a different
temperament from Ferdinand, acted in so gross
a manner that his atrocities roused the anger of
the Chinese. If the early European traders who
went to China had been honourable men like
Ferdinand Andrade, intercourse with the Far
East might have been of an entirely different
character. It was the buccaneering spirit of
the Portuguese and Dutch, as well perhaps as
the later forceful methods of the English, which
closed China to the West. Simon Andrade ' was

obliged to flee, 1520, probably with a large booty, including children carried off into slavery.'

Simon's conduct imperilled the safety of the Portuguese envoy and his staff in China. The envoy reached Nanking, where he found the Emperor and, unhappily for him, at the same time an envoy from the King of Bantam, appealing to the Emperor to save him from Portuguese aggression. It was not till 1521 that Pirez reached Peking, only to be ordered back to Canton, where he arrived 22nd September. In the summer preceding, two more Portuguese flotillas reached Port Namoa ; but the Chinese ordered them away and, on their refusal, attacked, burning some of the ships and seizing a number of Portuguese, whom they cast into prison. The envoy Pirez and his staff suffered a like fate in Canton. All but five died of torture, hunger, or disease. In 1522 another flotilla was attacked by the Chinese, when many Portuguese perished.

Later a settlement was founded at Ningpo which evidently became very prosperous ; but ' the exactions of the Portuguese and their massacre of Chinese aroused the latter, who destroyed the settlement in 1545. It is said that 12,000 " Christians," of whom 800 were Portuguese, were destroyed and 80 ships or junks burnt.' A similar revolt took place against the Portuguese settlement in the province of Fukien at Ch'üan-chow in 1549.

Undismayed, the Portuguese still continued to trade in the southern Chinese islands and finally, about 1550 or later, secured a footing at Macao, a rocky peninsula at the mouth of the Canton River. They are said to have obtained this *pied à terre* through their aid in destroying pirates, who occupied islands called accordingly by the Portuguese the Ladrones. It was in a grotto on this peninsula that Camoens wrote part of his *Lusiad*, thereby becoming the father of Portuguese literature.

For Portuguese excesses against their enemies, the Moslems, under whom they had suffered so long, there may be excuse. For Spanish atrocities in the East there can be none, except that as heirs of centuries of Moslem rule, their blood had been infected with a like poison. For da Gama and d'Almeida against the Moslems something may be said ; for Simon de Andrade, and many others of his kind, against Chinese and natives of southern lands, no extenuation can be made. But that a country of only two million people— soon after greatly reduced by the Plague—like Portugal should dare to go forth ' to hold the gorgeous East in fee ' was a feat worthy of the Lusiads.

The Spaniards. When Columbus the Italian, whom the Portuguese lost to Spain, set out on his voyages of discovery, it was to search for the western passage to China and the Indies. He found the mainland of America and, using Marco

Polo's term, called it Ciamba (Champa, part of Cambodia and Annam), but sought vainly for the Cattigara passage.   Magellan rounded Cape Horn in 1520 and led the way westward to the East. Miguel Lopez de Legazpi set out from Mexico in 1564 with four ships, seized the Luzon Islands in 1571, calling them the Philippines, and founded Manila, which remained Spanish till 1898, after the war with the United States.   For over 300 years this was the centre of Spanish influence in the Far East.

In 1575 a promising attempt to open trade with China was ruined through the foolish ignoring of a Chinese envoy by the Spanish governor. This despite resulted in terrible suffering to the missionaries who accompanied the envoy on his return to China.   Attempts were vainly made by Spanish Augustins, Franciscans and Dominicans to enter China ; though some found a temporary abode in Macao.   Attempts at direct trade being unsuccessful, the Spaniards obtained a footing in 1626 on the island of Formosa, not then under Chinese rule.   From this they traded chiefly with Japan, but from it they were driven in 1642 by the Dutch.   As there was considerable junk traffic between China and Manila, the Spaniards in 1669 secured some regulation of commerce between Ningpo, Canton, Macao and Manila. Curiously, though their trade with China was small, they introduced their Spanish dollar, which later became the Mexican dollar, flaunting its cap of Liberty before a nation unversed in such a symbol; this dollar became the chief medium of currency along the coast, for the only Chinese minted money was the copper cash. Spanish relations with China were ' disfigured by two great massacres of Chinese in the Philippines. In 1602 there were 20,000 Chinese in Manila and only 800 Spaniards.' Suspected of plots, the Chinese were nearly all killed. In 1639 out of 33,000 Chinese there, 22,000 in like manner perished. Such were the epic and heroic Spaniards and Portuguese, lauded by M. Cordier to the detriment of the ' prudent Dutch and English traders who dispossessed them, whose counting-house was their fortress.'

The Dutch. As to the Dutch, they began in 1584 to search for a northern passage to China and the Indies. Desiring to curb this ambition, Philip II of Portugal seized all their ships at Lisbon which were trading between Lisbon and Holland. So jealous an act determined the Dutch to seek their own markets in the East, and to be no longer dependent on the Portuguese. They first succeeded, 1595-7, by reaching the Moluccas, then Bantam in Java, in which island they founded Batavia in 1619, and it has ever since been theirs. It is well to remember that with all these southern islands China had long been connected by trade and tribute, and that the Chinese are to-day the most important part of their population.

The Dutch in 1622 attempted to seize Macao from the Portuguese, and would have succeeded but for the accidental explosion of their powder barrels. Instead they occupied the Pescadore Islands between Formosa and China; but the Chinese refused to deal with them till they had evacuated those islands for Formosa, not then Chinese territory. This evacuation was made, and trade was begun both with China and Japan. Four years later, in 1626, the Spanish settled in the north of Formosa, from which the Dutch drove them in 1642. Twenty years later, 1661-2, Koxinga, the Chinese corsair defender of the Ming dynasty, drove the Dutch out of Formosa. After that, in spite of humiliating embassies to Peking, their intercourse with China became of a sporadic nature.

The Dutch in their sacrifice of honour for the sake of gain in China—referred to later—have won no admiration from friend or foe, and there is much truth in M. Cordier's acid comment: ' Never do we see the directional counsels of the Dutch penetrated with a noble or disinterested idea; they sacrificed all, friend and enemy, even religion . . . for the sake of their profit. Dutch colonial history is a fine page in the history of European commercial development, but a villainous page in the history of humanity.' Yet after all, the crimes of Protestant Holland were trifling compared with the ferocities of Spain and Portugal, with which he unfavourably contrasts it.

The Russians. Russian intercourse with the Far East began with the Mongol uprising. As Mongol power declined, the power of Russia arose, and soon there began that slow but sure Muscovite march eastward which has added Siberia, that is more than half of Asia, though still empty, to its greater half of Europe.

Relations with China under the Ming dynasty were attempted in 1567 and 1619 and under the Manchus in 1654, 1657, 1670, 1675 and 1688, but the honourable refusal of the Russian envoys to kotow—unlike the Dutch—prevented success.

The Treaty of Nertchinsk, in 1689, laid the foundation of Russia's future intercourse with China, by which trade was permitted under stringent regulations. Later, in 1721, an embassage obtained permission for a mission to settle in Peking. It was partly ecclesiastical (for the sake of certain Russian prisoners there), partly diplomatic. With this embassage there travelled Dr. John Bell of Antermony, Scotland, who in 1763 published his *Travels from St. Petersburg in Russia to divers parts of Asia.* In 1727 the boundaries were fixed, and 200 Russian merchants allowed to visit Peking every two years. In 1733 the Manchus sent their first embassy abroad—to Moscow.

The United States of America began its relations with China, as an independent nation, in February 1784. The sailing ship, the *Empress of China*, commanded by Capt. Green, sailed from

New York in that month and reached Canton on 28th August. It carried chiefly a cargo of ginseng, a tonic root abundant in America, in which the Chinese have great confidence. Major Samuel Shaw acted as supercargo. On the way he was welcomed, in the Straits of Sunda, by the officers of two French warships, and with them travelled to Macao. He was well received on reaching Canton by English, French, Danes and Dutch. Returning to America, he was given a post as secretary in the War Office, received the thanks of Congress for the report of his voyage, and was sent out again in 1786, duly appointed by Congress as its first ' Consul ' to China.

During ' the first decade of the nineteenth century the imports to China in American bottoms amounted to £1,000,000 and exports to little less.' The American ' clipper ' ships soon rivalled the British and successfully competed for the carrying trade, even with British ports. The middle of the century saw half the imports and exports conveyed in these ships. ' By 1865 the Americans had also the lion's share of the shipping on the Yang-tze—seven up-to-date steamers out of nine, besides others on the coast and Japan lines.' The American Civil War brought about a decline, aided also by the development in Britain of the iron steamship. Fifty years later, in 1914, the United States' tonnage was less than one per cent. of the whole in the ports of China and its trade but seven per cent. of the total amount. In consequence of the European War the tonnage rose to five per cent. and the trade to thirteen per cent.

It is worthy of note that the first British missionary to China, Robert Morrison, was under the necessity of travelling on an American ship in order to reach there. The East India Company, in whose employ he later found opportunity for doing his life's work, would not convey him.

If American trade with China has not of late years greatly developed, the opposite is the case with American Protestant Missions. These have been responsible for the larger half of the educational work of missions, as well as of the philanthropic work. American sympathy with China was shown by the calling of the Washington Conference, as also of the Opium Conference in Geneva, which latter would have been more successful if it had been less doctrinaire. Good from both will assuredly result.

The French. On the advent of the Austrians, Prussians, Danes and Swedes it is unnecessary here to dwell, and we may close this chapter with a reference to French intercourse and Roman Catholic Missions. France began her search for India and Cathay in 1503 by the southern route and failed. Again in 1523 an attempt was made northward. It was not till 1698 that the ' Compagnie de Chine ' was founded and the first ship, *l'Amphitrite*, was sent out. Commerce, however, received a deadly blow when the French King in 1716 forbade foreign importations of silks and stuffs in favour of home production, and caused the cargo of the ship *Grand Dauphin* to be burnt on its arrival—very ardent protectionism.

The chief interest of France has lain less in commerce than in its support of the Roman Catholic Missions. To this further attention will be drawn later. Here, more of interest will be found in a brief sketch of the work of the able and devoted missionaries of the Roman Church who, but for internal dissension, gave promise of converting China to Christianity in the seventeenth century.

Roman Catholic Missions. St. Francis Xavier, the Jesuit, styled by Urban VIII the ' Apostle to the Indies,' may rightly be considered the most fervent missionary to the East of the Western Church. He arrived at Goa in 1542, the same year that three Portuguese, driven by a typhoon, were the first authentic Europeans to land in Japan. After seven years of notable success in Southern India, Ceylon and the Malay Archipelago, St. Francis was the means of converting a Japanese at Malacca and went with him to preach the Gospel in Japan in 1549. During his two years' sojourn there—a time of serious political upheaval—it is said that some hundreds of thousands of Japanese embraced Christianity. But the magnet which ever drew this devoted apostle was China, for ' if the Chinese welcomed the Christian faith, the Japanese would have

little difficulty in abandoning their errors, which
had been communicated to them by the Chinese.'
Thwarted on the one hand by the jealous Portuguese governor of Malacca—whose excommunication he demanded—and on the other by the
Portuguese at Macao and the Chinese at Canton,
' white from his austerities and labours,' though
only forty-six years of age, he died of fever in a
wretched thatched hut on the island of Shang-
ch'uan (St. John's), 27th Nov., 1552. He was a
saint who served the common Western Church
before the Reformation, and whom all the world
of whatever creed may admire.

In Japan his successors found immediate though
short-lived prosperity, thanks to the liaison of
Christianity with a political party, whose defeat
resulted in the expulsion of Church and trade from
the country. His followers in China were to meet
with slower but more substantial success. It
has already been shown that the Spaniards—
Augustins, Franciscans, Dominicans—made unsuccessful attempts from the Philippines, the
Dominicans especially in 1587, 1590, 1596, 1598
and 1611. The last-named finally succeeded in
obtaining a footing in Fukien province from the
island of Formosa. As time passed they became
great opponents of the Jesuits and, by their
honesty and zeal, wrought havoc with the work
of the Church.

Macao, the Portuguese settlement, was made a
bishopric in 1557 ; but propagation of the Faith

was only begun from that point of vantage at a
later date and by Italian priests. One of these
was Michel Ruggiero, who landed in 1579, and
with P. Pasio founded the first station on the
mainland at Chao-ch'ing in Kuangtung, which
later was transferred by Ricci to Ch'ao-chow.
Another Jesuit, Valignani, known for his cry
' O rock ! O rock ! when wilt thou open ? '
was Ricci's inspirer and way-preparer.

It was he, Matteo Ricci, the Jesuit, who became
the actual founder of the Church in China.
Arriving at Macao in 1583, he settled first,
dressed as a Buddhist monk, at Chao-ch'ing, then
at Ch'ao-chow. In 1594 he changed his dress
to that of a Chinese scholar and made his way
overland to Nanking on the river Yang-tze.
Compelled to leave that great city, he settled for
a time at Nan-ch'ang, returned to Nanking in
1598, and with P. Cattaneo visited Peking.   In
1600 he set out again with P. Pantoja for Peking.
After several months' imprisonment in Tientsin,
they succeeded in reaching Peking, the capital
of the Ming emperor, on 4th Jan., 1601.   Ricci's
present of valuable clocks and other articles
proved acceptable to the emperor.   His acquaintance with the language enabled him also, in
proper style, to offer his knowledge of mathematics, astronomy, geography and other sciences
for the imperial service.   He gradually won the
confidence of numerous able scholars, some of
whom became Christians.   One of these rose to

the highest office in the land, and secured the
appointment of Ricci's successors as members
of the Board of Astronomy.   So diplomatic was
Ricci that ere long other Jesuits were allowed to
reside in China, and mission stations were opened
in several important centres.   Ricci remained
in Peking, Superior-General of the Jesuits in
China, till his death at fifty-nine in 1610.   He
produced mathematical and other treaties and
left behind, *inter alia*, a tractate still famous on
the existence of God.

It was his tact and ability, aided perhaps by
a decaying dynasty, which opened the way for
Jesuits, Dominicans, and Franciscans to settle in
various parts of China.   His tradition of learning
was maintained in Peking by a succession of
brilliant scholars, amongst whom was Adam
Schall, whose ability in astronomy and in the
founding of cannon made him acceptable to the
Manchu dynasty, which succeeded the Ming in
1644.   The position of Vice-President of the
Astronomical Board was held by Schall and his
successors until 1837.   Among them one of the
most noted was Verbiest.   In 1700 the French
King succeeded in securing the monopoly of
appointing missionaries to the Jesuit Mission in
Peking, and thereafter it was manned by French
scholarly priests such as de Fontaney, Bouvet,
Gerbillon, Visdelou and Le Comte.   It was from
this date that France became protector of Catholic
Missions in China.

The great Manchu Emperor K'ang Hsi showed every kindness to the Jesuits, and himself studied with them. That he was not opposed to their religion is evident from his granting liberty of propagation throughout the land. It was the controversy raised against the Jesuits by the Dominicans, in which the emperor's own judgment was challenged, that turned K'ang Hsi against Pope and Church. The Dominicans and Franciscans protested against the practices of the Jesuits; they objected to the term they used for God, to their permission of ancestor worship and the cult of Confucius, to their pandering to idolatry, to their casuistry and to their profitable trading. Such was the storm which started the avalanche of distrust that ultimately swept the priests out of the land, save the few who were useful as astronomers.

The appeal to the Pope made by the Dominicans and the Franciscans—who owed their very existence in China to the Jesuits—brought decisions from him and later from his successors which first contravened, then approved and finally repudiated the positions taken by the Jesuits. Had this dispute been kept as a domestic matter it might have done little harm. But the Jesuits had invited the Emperor K'ang Hsi, himself a scholar of high repute, to give his judgment on the meaning of certain religious terms and ceremonies. His judgment coincided with their practices—yet the Bulls of Popes, who knew no Chinese at all,

and of Dominican bishops, who were scarcely able
to read any, actually denied the accuracy of His
Majesty's interpretation of his own language and
customs ! Here was an *imperium in imperio*,
as intolerable to the great Emperor of China as
it was to certain Western rulers ! Finally, after
a century of controversy, in 1742 the Jesuit
stronghold was stormed and overthrown by a
Papal Bull. Thirty years later, in 1773, the
Jesuit Order itself was suppressed by Clement
XIV, which resulted in the excommunication
and persecution of Jesuits in China by their
co-religionists. When in 1715 Clement XI first
published a Bull condemning the Jesuit practices,
the Emperor K'ang Hsi riposted in 1717 by
proscribing Christianity in the empire, and by
deporting the Dominicans ; some persecution of
their converts broke out, which later was abated.
When the great K'ang Hsi died and his son Yung
Cheng succeeded to the throne in 1723, the latter
commenced a definite suppression of Christianity,
and in 1724 publicly proscribed it. The foreign
priests, save the scientists in Peking, were driven
to Macao, some suffering cruel treatment ; Christian altars were destroyed, the churches turned
into schools and faithful native converts perse-
cuted. Nevertheless, it is a Roman priest who,
while deploring Yung Cheng's alienation from
Christianity, spoke highly of his noble character
as a sovereign. His greater successor, Ch'ien
Lung, was also a persecutor of the Church. The

proscription by his predecessor had not been thoroughly pressed home. In 1784—eleven years after the suppression by the Pope of the Jesuits— a more serious repression of Christianity took place in China. Bishops and priests were cast into prison ; seven died there. Several had been martyred in Fukien in 1747. Others were deported. None were allowed to remain in China, save those useful as scientists in Peking. When the first fury was over, some of the priests bravely visited their flocks in secrecy. But the eighteenth century closed with the Jesuits in China disbanded, and the Church apparently destroyed.

It is to the Jesuits that China owed the revision of its calendar, the mapping of the country, improved mathematical knowledge and an introduction to other Western sciences. Their contribution to Western knowledge was also of great value ; for their records and publications form the basis of subsequent sinology and Western knowledge in general of China.

The Jesuits were of course—Jesuits ; the Dominicans and Franciscans honest fanatics. Whether the tactfulness of the Jesuits would have succeeded where fanatical honesty was doomed to failure, who shall say ? Perhaps even in religion honesty is the best policy !

VIII

ENGLISH TRADING RELATIONS

THE eighteenth century closed in the Far East with China at the zenith of its expansion. From the Pacific on the east, including Korea, Formosa and the Loochoo Islands, as far as and including Tibet, Nepal, and Turkestan on the west ; from the borders of Siberia in the north to and including Cochin-China on the south, the Emperor Ch'ien Lung was everywhere acknowledged as supreme lord.

In the West the nineteenth century opened with a volcanic eruption in Europe which scattered its ashes as far as China. The revolution in France and the Napoleonic Wars poured their miseries over Europe. They darkened also the sky of European development in China. This catastrophe might well have absorbed all the attention of Britain ; but that country still had its representatives abroad, and its commerce, essential even to war, must be maintained.

In the midst of these European turmoils, in 1804, George III sent a letter to the Emperor of China telling of the wicked revolutionaries in France and the uprising of a vile person (Napoleon) as its ruler. The object of his letter was to close the door of China to the French, who still had certain ships in the Indian Ocean—just one of those diplomacies which nations feel justified in using in war, but which private individuals shun in times of peace. The Emperor graciously received the King of England's presents, really as 'tribute,' and sent a reply as from a chief to his vassal :

'Your Majesty's kingdom is at a remote distance beyond the seas, but is observant of its duties and obedient to our law, beholding from afar the glory of our Empire and respectfully admiring the perfection of our Government. Your Majesty has despatched messengers with letters for our perusal and consideration. We find that they are dictated by appropriate sentiments of esteem and veneration, and being therefore inclined to fulfil the wishes and expectations of your Majesty we have determined to accept the whole of the accompanying offering.

'With regard to those of your Majesty's subjects, who for a long course of years have been in the habit of trading to our Empire, we must observe to you that our Celestial Empire Government regards all persons and nations with eyes of charity and benevolence, and always treats and considers your subjects with the utmost indulgence and affection. On their account therefore there can be no place or occasion for any effort on the part of your Majesty's Government.'

This letter was thoroughly typical of China's attitude towards foreigners, then and for a century afterwards, to the undoing of the dynasty.

In 1802, so as to prevent Macao from falling into the hands of the French, to the great danger of our valuable trade with China, the British occupied it, but later withdrew. In 1808, in collusion with our then allies, the Portuguese, the British landed reinforcements. This aroused Chinese ire; for they claimed Macao as Chinese territory, and the Portuguese were pledged not to admit any foreign troops without their consent. Conseqntly the Chinese, adopting the course which either side adopted when angry, suspended trade. Admiral Drury, whose application for an interview had been refused by the Canton Viceroy, determined to seek one. Arming all his boats he set out for Canton; the Chinese forts opened fire on him, wounding one of his men; he made a signal to attack, but his boats failed to observe it; in the interests of peace he decided not to repeat the signal and withdrew. A pagoda was built by the Chinese to commemorate the ' victory ' they had obtained over the English— almost a bloodless one !

It was in the same year that one of the world's greatest evolutionary forces entered China, in the shape of Protestant Missions. Robert Morrison landed at Canton.

All British trade was then under the control of the East India Company. Independent trading

vessels, known as ' country ships,' only carried
on business under the Company's permits. While
hindering freedom of trade, this arrangement had
certain advantages in dealing with such an
uncertain government as that of China; for,
during a difficult and dangerous period, it
centralized authority in a great and responsible
trading concern, rather than in a foreign government official, with whom indeed the Chinese would
have refused to deal. The Chinese people were
willing enough to trade; but the policy of their
government was to keep foreign trade under
strict control—as America does in a different
way by its exclusive tariffs. Consequently, powerful though John Company might be, and lucrative
the trade both to buyer and seller, the Chinese
Government kept the Company and all foreign
traders cooped up in a virtual prison. This lay
in a narrow strip—the Shameen—just outside
the city gate of Canton. It was a veritable
Ghetto, but worse; for the gates of this Ghetto
were perpetually closed against entry by foreigners
into the city or country.

Unable to obtain civilized recognition by the
officials and government, forbidden to address
to them communications in Chinese, limited to
the form of the ' humble petition,' prohibited
from learning the language under penalty of
death to the native teacher, treated as and
officially styled ' barbarians,' confined to the
pestilential overcrowded suburb of an almost

tropical city—it is astonishing that foreigners still persisted in hoping for human conditions.

In 1814, with the appointment by the Company of Sir George Staunton as Superintendent, an attempt was made to obtain amelioration of these hardships. Meeting with overbearing resistance on the part of the Viceroy, Staunton ordered the withdrawal of all the British from Canton. The Viceroy thereupon agreed to discuss terms, when one of the most valuable points gained was the right of communicating in the Chinese language, instead of through imperfectly educated native linguists, though all communications must still take the form of the ' humble petition.'

Twenty years had now passed since the Macartney embassage. Under the advice of Sir George Staunton and his associates, the British Government decided to make a further attempt to reach the Central Government. The object of such approach would be to secure better conditions of trade, through such civilized inter-relationship between the two governments as existed between all civilized nations.

In due course Lord Amherst was appointed and sailed with his staff on the *Alceste*, Feb. 8, 1816. Having reached Tientsin he was escorted to Peking in official barges which, as before, bore the humiliating ensign 'Tribute bearer,' for England was included in the Manchu list of vassal or tributary countries.

The visit of Lord Amherst unhappily coincided

with our war with the Gurkhas in India. The Chinese had invaded Nepal on a punitory expedition against the Gurkhas in 1790, in consequence of the latter's invasion of Tibet. The campaign, amid impassable mountains, was brilliantly carried out ; the Gurkhas were beaten and acknowledged China's sovereignty. The British Government in India had rendered aid to the Chinese against the Gurkhas, an aid which was of value to the Macartney expedition. But now, in 1816, the British had made its conquest of Nepal, a conquest naturally resented by the Chinese suzerain, and not therefore helpful to Lord Amherst's mission. Amongst others who accompanied him to Peking were Sir George Staunton, (Sir) John Francis Davis, and Robert Morrison of the London Missionary Society, who acted as interpreter.

Arriving at the Summer Palace at five o'clock in the morning, after an exhausting all night journey, Lord Amherst was called upon, even hauled and pushed, to present himself, unwashed and dishevelled, without his credentials or court robes, before the Emperor. This he declined to do as unseemly in a representative of the King of England, as well as discourteous to the Emperor of China ; moreover the day following had previously been fixed for the audience. Peremptorily he and his party were dismissed and turned away the same day.

What was the reason for this discourtesy ? It all arose over the kotow, symbol of vassalage.

The kotow and the spirit behind it were the cause of our subsequent wars with China. How could a self-respecting nation permit the representative of its sovereign to kotow, or prostrate himself, before the Chinese Emperor ? To do so was to acknowledge the emperor as overlord and one's own sovereign as his subject. The Dutch kotowed the requisite nine times and were treated with the contempt they earned. The Russians refused, made little progress, but were respected. In the case of Lord Amherst, the officials had been ordered to instruct him on his arrival in the court etiquette of the kotow, a procedure usual with vassal envoys. His refusal put them in a difficulty, as they had assured their sovereign that the barbarian would make the usual obeisance. Their master, Chia Ch'ing, ignorant, cruel and dissolute, had no knowledge of Britain save that it was a long way off and its people manifestly crude barbarians. To the letter from the English king, brought by Lord Amherst, the Emperor sent a most haughty reply written in Manchu, Chinese and Latin, complaining of the disrespect shown by the ambassador, but still condescending to accept the king's ' tribute.' He also sent return presents, including a Ju-i, or baton of delegated authority, but told the king :

' The Celestial Court does not value things from. afar, and curious or ingenious things from his (the King's) country have no special value.' He bids the English king keep peace among his people, and see to the security of his territory without relaxation. As to the future, he relieves him of the necessity of sending further envoys. ' Know,' he says, ' only to show the sincerity of your heart and study goodwill, and one can then say, without the necessity of sending annual representatives to my Court, that you progress towards civilized transformation. It is to the end that you continue your obedience that I send you this Imperial command ! ' That expresses with sufficient clearness the attitude of the supreme authority claimed by China over His Insignificance of England.

The Amherst embassy proved a complete failure, except to confirm the opinion already being reluctantly formed, that only three possibilities were open to the British—a resort to force, absolute submission to tyranny, or abandonment of the trade.

A similar difficulty had arisen with a special embassy sent by Alexander I of Russia in 1805. The envoy reached Urga in Mongolia ; but on his refusing to kotow, after four months of vain negotiation, a letter from Peking dismissed him in a humilating manner. This was the eleventh Russian embassy to China, and it accomplished nothing. The first Russian ship to travel round the world was the *Neva*. It visited Macao in 1796 and was able to dispose of a considerable cargo of furs there ; but orders were immediately received from Peking that no more Russian ships were to be admitted.

The failure of the Amherst Mission did not tend to ameliorate conditions in Canton. With imperial example before them, the authorities in that city were only prevented from extremes because of the fat purses they received from the Chinese traders, as well as the levies they made on the foreigners.

The charter of the East India Company was due to expire in 1834, and the British Government decided not to renew it, but to allow freedom of trade and enthrone 'competition.' The trade with China, at first, was a monopoly of the Company ; but, as already mentioned, independent traders had been allowed to do business in Canton under the licence of the Company, which was responsible to the Chinese for them. All trade was done with a committee of native merchants called the Co-Hong, who were responsible as a body for the payment of all balances due. Now that the powers of the East India Company were to be annulled, a question of revolutionary importance arose, namely, what was to be the future British authority in the port of Canton ?—the only port in which trade was permitted.

The Chinese officials on hearing of the contemplated change firmly declined to alter the old arrangement. The vassal King of England might please himself whom he sent, they would only deal according to the old system and would still hold communications with the head of the East India Company alone.   The reason for this was clear.   Under the old system the Chinese Government was only dealing with traders.   Under the proposed new system, it would be acknowledging and dealing with a royal representative— the very thing it was resolved not to do.

Nevertheless, it was essential for the British Government to take official control over its people trading with China, in order to see that they acted justly and received justice.   Consequently, shortly before the expiry of the charter, Lord Napier was, in December 1833, appointed Superintendent of Trade in China—a modest enough title !   He sailed for China, taking his wife and daughters to Macao.   John Francis Davis became his second in command, Robert Morrison his interpreter, and Capt. Charles Elliot, R.N., was on his staff.   His instructions were: 'Announce your arrival at Canton by letters to the Viceroy.   In addition to the duty of protecting and fostering the trade of His Majesty's subjects with the port of Canton, it will be one of your principal objects to ascertain whether it may not be practicable to extend that trade to other parts of the Chinese dominions.   And for this end you will omit no favourable opportunity of encouraging any disposition which you may discover in the Chinese authorities to enter into commercial relations with His Majesty's

Government.   It is obvious, with a view to the
attainment of this object, the establishment of
direct communications with the Imperial Court
at Peking would be desirable ;   and you will
accordingly direct your attention to discover
the best means of preparing the way for such
communications '—and so on.

The arrival of Lord Napier at Macao was
immediately reported by the local Chinese naval
officer to the Viceroy, who was thus placed in a
difficult position.   Here was a ' barbarian eye,'
that is a head or supervisor, of high rank.   To
refuse him might mean trouble.   To receive him
would be to change the whole existing relations,
for he would then have to deal with one who
would demand equality of standing.   Moreover,
he, the Viceroy, had no imperial authority to make
such a change, and independent action might
result in his own dismissal.   It would be unjust
in us not to consider the Chinese side equally
with our own.   He decided to issue an edict—
everything was done by edict, *de haut en bas*—
ordering the Co-Hong, the Chinese Committee of
Merchants, to inform the ' barbarian eye ' that
none but authorized traders could be admitted
to the port of Canton until the Throne had given
permission.   If Lord Napier wished to come he
must first send in a ' petition ' through the usual
channel, when the Throne would be memorialized
for instructions.

It was impossible for Lord Napier to ' petition '

and thus become a supplicant before a minor subordinate of the Viceroy. 'A man of broad sympathies, generous views and high courage,' he yet saw no way out of the difficulty but to obey the instructions of his own government. Accordingly, without applying for a permit, he sailed for Canton, took up his residence in the British factory, hoisted his flag, and sent a letter to the Viceroy announcing his arrival, courteously asking him for the honour of a personal interview. Mr. Astell carried the letter to the city gate, patiently bore the indignities he had to undergo, was interviewed by many officials ; but one and all—obedient of course to vice-regal instructions —refused to receive and forward the letter. Again the Viceroy issued an edict requiring the ' barbarian eye ' to leave Canton as soon as his ' commercial business ' was finished. Here are quotations from the edict : ' As to the object of the barbarian eye's coming to Canton it is for commercial business. The Celestial Empire appoints officers—civil ones to rule the people, military ones to intimidate the wicked. The petty affairs of commerce are to be directed by the merchants themselves. The officials have nothing to hear on the subject. . . . The great ministers of the Celestial Empire are not permitted to have intercourse by letters with outside barbarians. If the said barbarian eye throws in private letters, I, the Viceroy, will not at all receive or look at them.'

Edict after edict was issued ordering Lord Napier's withdrawal. The Viceroy also reported to the Throne that ' the " barbarian eye " had actually sent a letter to your Majesty's minister, Lu (meaning himself), bearing on its face the forms and styles of equality, together with the absurd characters Ta Ying Kuo, " Great Britain." ' He says ' it is plain, on the least reflection, that in order to distinguish the Chinese from outsiders it is of the utmost importance to maintain dignity and sovereignty. . . . Yet this barbarian eye . . . suddenly comes to the barbarian factories outside the city, and presumes to desire intercourse to and fro by official documents and letters with the officers of the Central Flowery Land ; this is, indeed, far beyond the bounds of reason.'

Perhaps his absurdest edict was that which contained the following statements : ' It would be most right immediately to put a stop to trade, but considering that the said nation's King has hitherto been in the highest degree reverently obedient, he cannot in sending Lord Napier at this time have desired him thus obstinately to resist.' The duties collected ' concern not the Celestial Empire to the extent of a hair or a feather's down. The possession or absence of them is utterly undeserving of a careful thought. Their broadcloths and camlets are still less important, and of no regard. But the tea, the rhubarb, the raw silk of the Central Land are the sources by which the said nation's people live and maintain their life. For the fault of one man, Lord Napier, must the livelihood of the whole nation be cut off ? ' So the Viceroy, filled with pity for the wretched barbarian, would not destroy Great Britain at one fell blow by cutting off its ' turkey rhubarb, its tea and its silk.'

He soon, however, stopped all trade and ordered all Chinese employees to leave their foreign employers. In addition, thousands of candidates for the civil and military triennial examinations had arrived. Anti-foreign feeling found bitter expression, and the situation was threatening. Lord Napier, availing himself of the presence of two British cruisers in the lower harbour, ordered them up to Canton for protection. They were fired on by the forts, two British being killed. The fire was returned and the ships reached the Canton anchorage.

It is probable that, despite his bombastic edict issued in reply to Lord Napier's strong action, the Viceroy would have become more amenable ; but already, on August 1, Lord Napier had lost by death his invaluable interpreter, Dr. Morrison, and now he himself became seriously ill with fever. At this critical juncture in the state of political affairs, Lord Napier's condition became so precarious that his doctor ordered his removal to Macao. Delay in the issue of the necessary passport, and misconduct on the part of the officials, kept Lord Napier seven more days in the heat of a Cantonese August. He reached Macao, but never recovered, and died October 11, 1834. Had he lived, the knowledge he had acquired of official character, as well as his own fine spirit, might have prevented the so-called ' Opium War.' That he had grasped the situation and would have dealt wisely with it seems evident from his letter to Lord Palmerston of August 14.

On his death the Viceroy reopened trade ; but his anxiety lest individual traders should take the law into their own hands is shown by his immediately requiring the merchants to appoint a temporary *t'ai pan*, or head, and write home for the appointment of a permanent one, demanding nevertheless that he must be a merchant to deal with merchants, not a ' barbarian eye ' to deal with officials.

In the meantime the Emperor was very angry that Lord Napier's two small gunboats should be able to reduce his forts. He degraded everybody responsible, from the Viceroy downwards, and ordered methods by which the two gunboats should be hemmed in, and burnt by fireships, saying ' the beast will then be taken, the fish caught.' The imperial edict is more bombastic if possible than were those of the Viceroy. ' The barbarian eye must tremble and quake before my Celestial Majesty and be penitentially stimulated to awed submission.'

Mr. John Francis Davis succeeded Lord Napier ;

but, tied by his orders, resolved on a policy of quiescence, awaiting instructions from home. The British merchants petitioned their government, urging that quiet submission to insult and contemptuous treatment would only further compromise the national honour, and deploring that Lord Napier had not been substantially supported by armed forces. Lord Napier himself had written that, if pacific means continued unavailing, the destruction of forts and batteries along the coast would not be difficult. By that means the area of suffering would be limited and the lesson come home effectively to the government. The Duke of Wellington, however, replied : ' It is not by force and violence that His Majesty intends to establish a commercial intercourse between his subjects and China, but by the other conciliatory measures so strongly inculcated in all the instructions which you have received.'

Davis resigned and went home. After his departure matters in Canton only went from bad to worse. The *Argyle* had to put into a Chinese port for shelter. Twelve of her men were seized and held for ransom. An attempt at redress in Canton only resulted in insult to the British representative. The British Government, intent then and always on peace with China, swallowed the insult and ignored the matter.

IX

OPIUM AND THE OPIUM WAR

WE now reach the much debated question of Opium and the so-called ' Opium War.' Opium was not a new thing in China. It was known as early as the seventh century A.D., and was probably styled *a-fu-yung* in the fifteenth from the Arab *afyun*. Later it became *ya-p'ien*, probably direct from the word opium. Before the nineteenth century little was grown in China, and the amount annually imported was trifling. Until early in the seventeenth century it had only been taken by the mouth as a drug.

The smoking of opium was introduced by the Dutch between 1624-1662, as tobacco smoking had been but recently introduced by the Spaniards. The latter reached Formosa via the Philippines, arriving there from America. Having themselves adopted the West Indian habit of tobacco smoking, the Spaniards introduced tobacco into Formosa, whence the plant and the habit spread to China, Japan, indeed all over the Far East. In China the habit is now universal. Dr. Morse, speaking somewhat freely, says : ' Every man, woman and weaned child in China is a tobacco-smoker.' Opium-smoking was introduced by the Dutch from Java, where, as a cure for the malaria from which they suffered, they began to mix opium and arsenic with tobacco and smoke it in an ordinary pipe. They brought the habit with them to Formosa, whence it soon spread to the mainland through Amoy. The modern opium pipe is apparently a Chinese invention, and it is probable that opium has only been smoked alone without admixture since about 1800.

As early as 1589 opium was a recognized article of import, and had probably first been imported by the Arabs. It was, however, the Portuguese who, in the middle of the seventeenth century, availed themselves of the demand to import the supply. It was a profitable trade, and they kept it in their hands for over a century till 1773, when the East India Company came into competition. Tobacco was fulminated against as vigorously by the early Manchu rulers as by our King James. So was it with opium-smoking, though opium as a drug continued on the customs tariff as a legitimate article of medicine. It was the evil habit of smoking that the court opposed. The first anti-opium edict was issued in 1729, ordaining severe penalties against the sale of opium for smoking and against opium divans. At that time the total annual importation was the comparatively trifling amount of 200 chests. By 1773—fifty years later—this number had increased to a thousand chests. It was in that year that the East India Company, in order to prevent further conflicts in India amongst traders of various foreign nations, assumed there the control of opium production and sale. For seven years, 1773-1780, private British traders bought opium from the Company and elsewhere and competed in the trade with the Portuguese, when the East India Company finally decided to make the China trade its own monopoly. In ten years, by 1790, the import increased over fourfold to 4054 chests. As the vice was making itself specially noticeable in Canton, in 1796 the Emperor emphasized the preceding edicts, increasing their penalties. In 1800 appeared the first edict entirely prohibiting both the import of opium and the home cultivation. Up to that date opium had been a normal import like cloth or any other article of trade.

In obedience to this edict the East India Company and the Co-Hong (*i.e.* the official Chinese merchants) ceased to traffic in the drug in China, but tried in vain to stop the import by foreign ships. China was not the only market for opium, and private traders were entitled to buy opium not only in India but elsewhere. There was plenty to be had. In China there was a growing demand, plenty of foreigners and of ships able to supply it, as well as any number of Chinese officials to encourage them. True, the higher Chinese officials stipulated for a bond from every ship arriving in the port of Canton that it was

free from opium, but had no hesitation in con-
niving at Chinese traders finding a way out of the
difficulty—for a satisfying consideration. Consequently the opium, instead of being brought
in on the ship, was discharged into Chinese boats
just outside the port limit, thus enabling the
foreign sailing ships to acquire a clean bill. From
1790 to 1821 the import went on under worse
conditions than before the edict, the average
annual import being something under 5000 chests.
All the nations carried on the trade. The United
States were just as deep in it as the British, for
American boats carried all the Turkey opium
imported.

So far as prohibition was concerned, the
Emperor by issuing the edict had done his duty;
the Viceroy by publishing it had done his ; the
Co-hong and East India Company by observing
it had done theirs ; and the tribe of officials and
private merchants, Chinese and foreign, by seeing
that the smokers were provided with the drug,
did theirs ! Otherwise, for twenty years the
edict was a dead letter. By the judicious use of
baksheesh—not by the foreign trader, but by
the Chinese themselves—all eyes were closed,
even those on preventive and guard boats lying
alongside the importing ship.

In 1821 the thieves fell out ; in other words, a
quarrel arose amongst the Chinese officials over
the sharing of the spoil. The Viceroy, who had
always been well acquainted with the system,

had to punish someone, so mulcted the innocent
senior Chinese Hong merchant in a heavy fine
and warned the three principal foreign merchants,
innocent and guilty, British, American and Portuguese, that the edict would be rigidly enforced.
In consequence, the Chinese traders arranged to
ensure a clean bill for the foreign ships outside
Chinese jurisdiction, or at any rate supervision ;
the ships now discharged their opium into fast
armed galleys built by the Chinese traders for
the purpose and rowed by fifty to seventy men.
Later still, permanent receiving ships were
anchored outside—at Lintin—to take delivery of
the discharged opium, which the Chinese then
' smuggled ' along the coast. Everybody con-
nived at it, and the trade between 1821-28 grew
from 4494 to 9708 chests. From 1828 smuggling
was no longer confined to Chinese vessels, for
foreign ships began to carry the opium along the
coast. For instance, the American schooner *Rose*
dropped anchor at Namoa near the commodore's
flag-ship. He came on board, read an imperial
edict forbidding trade, after which followed the
private interview—' How many chests have you
on board ? ' and so on. On his departure the
Chinese buyers came on board and transhipped
the opium to the satisfaction of everybody's
pocket, including the commodore's own and
that of his staff. By 1835 the 9708 chests had
grown to 18,712, and by 1839 to over 30,000
chests.

After the expiry of the East India Company's charter, trade became free and China, by its wanton treatment of Lord Napier, had refused the aid of an honourable man who would have befriended them in regard to this nefarious traffic.   There was no system of control over the numerous private venturers who were attracted by the immense profits to be made out of the noxious drug.   Soon there were large numbers of boats, foreign owned or under foreign control, plying as ' passenger boats.'   These boats ceased to bribe as the Chinese did, and consequently had to run the gauntlet of the guard boats, with not infrequent fighting.   Hitherto every Chinese official had received his price, and the stricter the ' prohibition ' the greater was the possibility of ' squeeze ' and profit.   Now, threatened with the loss of these ' insults,' the officials protested with shocked pens against the wicked trade. And a wicked trade it was.   We cannot justly apply the developed moral standard of to-day to that of even a century ago, when slave-raiding was neither illegal nor considered immoral.   Many believed they were conferring with opium a boon on the Chinese, as a prophylactic against and cure for the scourge of malaria.   We must remember that the largest amount ever imported—apart from the native product, which developed enormously later—may not have been excessive for legitimate use as a medicine over so large a population as that of China.   But the use was not legitimate, and the best English merchants avoided the traffic.

In June 1836 a very able petition was presented to the Throne by Hsü Nai-tsi, formerly Provincial Judge in Canton, then Vice-President of the Court Sacrifices, in which the whole situation was honestly and accurately described. He advocated legalisation of the traffic instead of useless prohibition, which seemed only to increase the traffic, a traffic which also had now begun to drain silver from the country. One reason why certain foreign merchants had encouraged the opium trade was that it helped to balance the increasing trade in silk and other exports Formerly they had to import silver; now opium turned the balance in their favour, but of course to the disadvantage of the Chinese who had to export silver. It was not only the moral and social sense of the Throne which was now disturbed, but also its economic sensitiveness.

The Viceroy at Canton was asked to report on the memorial of Hsü. He did so favourably. Immediately, the prohibitionist Chu Tsun, President of the Board of Rites, replied in an able memorial, pointing out that, if it were possible to licence, it was equally possible to prohibit. A suggestion had been made that the restrictions on the native cultivation of the drug should be relaxed; but he pointed out that already memorials had arrived from Fukien, Kuangtung, Chekiang, Shantung, Yunnan and Kueichow asking for

greater stringency against the cultivation. Here
we find the beginning—already acknowledged in
a third of the provinces of the country—of the
native cultivation of the poppy, which in time
painted the countryside in gorgeous colour. Chu
Tsun was rightly distressed over the matter. He
says : ' The influence of opium on commerce is,
however, of minor importance ; the chief objec-
tion to it is that it corrupts and enfeebles the
people ; and it is for that purpose that the
red-haired English have introduced it into China,
imitating in that respect the other red-haired
(the Dutch), who by means of it conquered Java.
Measures should be taken to guard against this
danger. . . . Opium is destroying the army, and
nothing short of total prohibition will save the
soldiers from ruin, and the officials and scholars
will share the same fate. The morals of the
common people, too, are low ; and if all restrain-
ing influence is removed, they will all be de-
bauched, and opium will become as their daily
meat and drink '—a prophecy which the end of
the century threatened to see approximately
realized.

Another memorial drew attention to the adverse
balance of trade produced by the importation of
opium, stating it to be over ten millions of taels
a year. The legalisation of the trade must lead
to impoverishment. The remedy was strict prohibition and stern procedure against nefarious
Chinese, while at the same time the foreign

merchants 'must also be made to write to their king, telling him that opium is a poison which is injuring the Chinese; that Chinese smugglers have been severely punished; that in consideration of the fact that they are barbarians and aliens, the government does not now sentence them to death; and that if the opium trade is altogether abandoned, they will be graciously released and allowed to trade as usual; but, if they again have store-ships and bring them here to entice the Chinese, their trade will be stopped entirely, and the resident foreigners of the nation at fault will assuredly be condemned to death. ... Furthermore, it is the practice of foreigners to ride in sedan chairs and hire Chinese to carry them, to live licentious lives, to indulge in acts of violence, and to break the laws in every way. Prompt measures should be adopted to check all these practices and to enforce the laws; and this, too, can best be done by executing the laws on the traitorous Chinese who abet them.'

The Viceroy of Canton was instructed to consult further on the matter and report. It was generally believed in Canton that the opium import would be legalized, and those merchants who dealt in the drug were looking for a large expansion in the trade. Capt. Elliot, who had now been appointed British Superintendent, was of the same opinion. It came therefore as somewhat of a shock when the Chinese Government began seriously to tackle the smugglers, and to take action against the foreigners. On November 23, 1836. an order was issued for the expulsion of nine foreigners (four English, three Parsee, one American, and one uncertain), not because they were opium-dealers, but as the most responsible merchants in the place, and therefore responsible, according to Chinese practice, for all the misdeeds of the other merchants. The order remained on record—that was all.

On June 22, 1837, the smuggling ' passenger boats ' were abolished in similar fashion ; on August 4 receiving ships were by imperial edict ordered away. Other ' final orders ' followed. Capt. Elliot was now, September 18, held responsible for all the misdeeds of everybody of whatever nationality, and chided in the usual superior fashion. He pointed out that he was only the British representative and that only for legitimate trade, possessing no powers in regard to opium. More than half the opium came from places outside British authority. The receiving ships, too, were American, French, Dutch, Spanish and Danish, besides English. The production and trade were international, and Capt. Elliot could not possibly undertake the required responsibility.

Repression and neglect followed each other to the confusion of everybody. Both courses were equally profitable to the corrupt mandarins. Opium divans were raided, reopened, raided. As a warning to foreigners, in December 1838 a dealer was seized and brought for execution by strangling in front of the Swedish 'hong' in the foreign 'factories.' A handful of foreigners protested and drove out the thousands of Chinese spectators. The Viceroy thereupon declared the factory settlement to be Chinese property, merely rented to the foreigners, and he therefore claimed the right to turn it into an execution ground as a warning to foreign opium traders. In the same month, December 18, 1838, Capt. Elliot ordered all illicit opium boats to leave the river, refusing protection to any British subject caught smuggling. Acting contrary to his instructions he even sent in a 'petition.' In this he asked the Viceroy for aid against the smuggling boats which had not obeyed his instructions. The Viceroy, happy in having brought the Superintendent to his knees, ordered the execution of another opium victim in front of the foreign abodes. No resistance was offered; but the flags of the British, American, French and Dutch were struck in protest, February 26, 1839, and it was long before they were broken again. Capt. Elliot again humiliated himself by sending a 'petition' to the Viceroy protesting against the insult, but the Viceroy contemptuously refused to look at it.

It is only fair to say that equal responsibility for the impasse lay on the British Government; for, despite the urgent appeal of Capt. Elliot— whose powers were severely limited—to decide on a definite policy, nothing whatever was done. On the other hand, the Emperor of China, Tao

Kuang, knew what he wanted ; he was genuinely distressed over the besotting of his people, he was alarmed by the spread of the baleful drug and was resolved on its prohibition. He stands forth as one of the noblest men of his country. He found a man of equal resolve in Lin Tse-hsü, whom he appointed High Commissioner to put an end to the poison. Unfortunately, nor need we blame them, they were both utterly supercilious towards the foreigner. To them everything outside China was barbarian. And their only knowledge of the barbarian was gathered from reports concerning the trader and sailor on their coasts !

The appointment of the High Commissioner Lin increased the alarm in the mandarin dovecotes of Canton, all well stocked with the golden eggs laid by the ill-omened opium vulture. He arrived March 10, 1839, and on the 18th ordered the delivery of all opium and demanded a bond that it would never again be imported. At the same time the Hoppo, or Chinese Superintendent of Trade, forbade any foreigner to leave the factories for Macao. This made prisoners of the foreigners. Communication with the ships was cut off, Chinese gunboats were collected in the river and armed troops assembled along the shore. The situation was of a threatening character.

The British merchants met on March 21, and decided almost unanimously against the opium traffic, offering to deliver up 1037 chests. This

amount Lin refused, and on March 22 sent
demanding Mr. Lancelot Dent, one of the leading
merchants. Though knowing he would be kept
as hostage, perhaps worse, he was willing to go ;
but the other merchants objected and demanded
a safe conduct and guarantee of safe return. Thus
was raised the question of extra-territoriality, now
so much discussed.

In the meantime Capt. Elliot had gone to
Macao and there ordered, March 22, all British
ships of every kind to assemble in Hongkong
Bay. He also wrote to the Viceroy, enquiring
the cause of the menacing warlike preparations.
So grave did the situation become, that, before
returning to Canton, he warned all British
subjects to be ready for immediate evacuation.
His return from Macao to Canton was perilous,
but he arrived safely, 24th, raised the British flag,
took Mr. Dent under his personal protection and
offered to take him in person to see the High
Commissioner on receiving a safe-conduct pass.
The Viceroy continued to close in upon the
factories and then ordered all the Chinese employees out of them. In these narrow quarters
were two to three hundred foreigners surrounded
by a triple cordon of troops and armed boats,
trumpets blowing and gongs braying unceasingly.

Strictly blockaded, deprived of food and water,
on the 25th Elliot demanded passports for all the
English ships and people to leave Canton. The
High Commissioner on the 26th demanded the

opium before he would issue passports, and sent repeated messages requiring instant obedience. On the 27th Elliot issued a notification under *force majeure*, demanding the delivery of all the opium of all British subjects, under guarantee of reimbursement by the British Government; 20,291 chests were delivered to the Chinese, of a value of two million and a half pounds. The High Commissioner made similar demands from American, French and Dutch merchants, whose trade in opium, he declared, had 'not been less than that of the English,' but he accepted the explanation that their stock was included in the English returns.

The bond he required against future opium traffic was a much more difficult matter. What he sought was a single neck to swing if necessary. But how could any merchant or group of merchants go bail for all comers of all nations ? His success had only emboldened him to humiliate still deeper his foe. Moreover, his demands would put all foreigners entirely at the mercy of unscrupulous mandarins. Capt. Elliot tore up the proposed bond. After six anxious weeks, on May 5 the triple cordon was removed, and passports issued, all save to sixteen persons, twelve English and four Parsee. Elliot refused to leave them, and again warned his fellow-countrymen to be ready to leave in a body.

A demand was now made that the sixteen merchants just referred to should sign a bond to

leave China and never return.   Under duress,
this bond was signed, on the instruction of Elliot.
On May 24 he and all the British left Canton for
Macao.   The opium was destroyed conscientiously
by the High Commissioner Lin on June 3 and
succeeding days, but in vain.   Though the British
representative and the navy gave no protection
or countenance to opium, the trade by no means
ceased.   A chest costing $500 before the destruc-
tion now fetched $1000, $1600, even $3000.   The
supply in China had been destroyed, but there
was more on the way, and soon the smuggling
became more vigorous than before.

The High Commissioner was now surprised
that trade in ' tea and rhubarb ' and other normal
commodities was not resumed at Canton ; but
Elliot had requested the merchants to do all their
trade at Macao until he received instructions from
Her Majesty's Government.   A Chinese proclamation commanding trade to be resumed at Canton
caused Elliot to reply.   After referring to the six
weeks of close confinement, he declared that ' the
traffic in opium has been chiefly encouraged and
protected by the highest officers in the empire
and that no portion of the foreign trade to China
has paid its fees to the officers with such regularity
as this of opium.'   He added that the destruction
of the opium had not destroyed the trade but
given it a further impulse, and the reason why
British ships did not proceed to Canton was
(*inter alia*) ' because there is no safety for a

handful of defenceless men in the grasp of the government at Canton; because it would be derogatory from the dignity of their sovereign and nation to forget all the insults and wrongs which have been perpetrated, till full justice be done, and till the whole trade and intercourse be placed upon a footing honourable and secure to this empire and to England.'

Matters were seriously complicated later by a party of sailors—perhaps both British and American—who at Kowloon raised a riot ' by their attempt to obtain spirits to drink; a shameful riot attended with unmanly outrage upon men, women and children, and the loss of innocent life.' Capt. Elliot himself gave $1500 to the family of the one Chinese who had been killed and tried the sailors, adjudging punishment; but the Chinese authorities demanded the guilty men and refused to recognize Elliot's right of judgment. Again, in less happy a cause was raised the question of extra-territoriality. The High Commissioner and the Viceroy now moved with troops against the British at Macao; all supplies were forbidden to them and their Chinese employees were ordered away. Fearing to compromise the Portuguese, Capt. Elliot embarked on Aug. 21, 1839. On the 24th the Portuguese Governor was ordered to expel the British; and in consequence, on the 26th, the British community set out for Hongkong harbour, men, women and children all alike being hurried from their residences, to seek a retreat on board their ships. The little fleet, consisting of small boats, schooners and lorchas, crowded with passengers, ' presented an affecting spectacle as it moved slowly away from the harbour.'

The refusal of Elliot to hand over the English sailors, for barbarous execution, produced a Chinese proclamation, ordering the people to arm themselves, oppose the British wherever they might land and seize them. Placards were also found in Hongkong ordering the wells to be poisoned, as in later years the community baker, without doubt well bribed, attempted to poison the whole community by putting a large quantity of arsenic in the bread. Supplies were soon stopped by Chinese guard boats, and Elliot had to fire on them before the willing people were allowed to bring food to the English market.

For months correspondence was carried on between Elliot and Lin, the High Commissioner, and one can only account for the almost submissive character of Elliot's letters by remembering that the British Government was bent on peace, and he was surrounded by merchants whose trade was being ruined. He ordered all ships having opium on board to leave Hongkong. He reported that all the sixteen merchants ordered to be deported were gone or going—save one, Mr. Matheson, for whom he begged consideration, which was refused. ' The vital demand was always for the surrender of the sailor who had murdered Lin Wei-hi '—a life for a life—indeed the demand was for all the men who had taken part in the fracas. ' Delay may draw down measures of extermination ' was the latest form of threat.

Elliot, supported by the merchants, had refused permission to British ship-captains to sign the bond demanded by Lin, a bond which would have submitted British subjects to capital punishment as well as confiscation of their ships, were opium found on board. A British ship, the *Thomas Coutts*, in consequence of legal advice that Elliot was acting *ultra vires*, sailed to Canton and gave the required bond. Ten days later, Commissioner Lin, encouraged by this submission, again demanded the surrender of the murderer of Lin Wei-hi, ordered the British ships at Hongkong either to come to Canton, or sail away within three days ' under penalty of complete destruction by fire.' This was followed by a notification that Chinese war vessels would be sent to seize all the offenders connected with the murder and with opium, as also all traitorous Chinese.

Elliot thereupon sailed for Canton with his two small gunboats to demand the withdrawal of this order. Threatened there by the oncoming Chinese fleet, orders were given to fire; four war-junks were sunk and the rest ' retired much damaged.'

Commissioner Lin, despite his excesses, commands respect for his single-mindedness. He had

one object in view, the riddance of his country
from opium. He had one simple but impossible
method of securing this, to attack the British
merchants and make them collectively responsible
for all comers, without distinction of nationality,
and subject always to confiscation and the death
penalty. He aimed at making the British responsible for the prevention of smuggling, not
only at Canton but all along the coast, a task
which the Chinese with all their ships and men
were unable to undertake. Though the Commissioner's demand was later somewhat modified,
he insisted that the British community must be
placed under Chinese law, a position to which
Great Britain could not—America did—submit
its people.

So far as the British Government was concerned,
it had substituted for the autocracy of the East
India Company a system of partial control under
a royally appointed Superintendent of Trade,
whom the Government left with instructions
which only accorded with its own indefinite state
of mind. The Superintendent did the best he
could according to his instructions, seeing all the
time that, however he might struggle to preserve
peace, war was inevitable. It was inevitable
because of the patriotic, impracticable, single-
track method of Commissioner Lin. It was
inevitable because Manchu vanity refused to
recognize any but tributary nations, who were
welcome to bask in the Manchu sun, at a distance,

so long as they submitted themselves to China's laws, prisons, tortures and execution ground.

The British Parliament was divided. The Government itself was for action ; the Opposition objected to support ' a vicious and demoralising traffic.' The British Chambers of Commerce thought it their duty to support the Government, not because they were interested in opium but because of the impossible conditions demanded, and on April 3, 1840, an Order in Council ordained reprisals, not war.

Commissioner Lin's letter to Queen Victoria saw only opium poisoning his people as the question in dispute. To the English and foreigners in general ' opium was an incident.' They had indeed devoted their opium to destruction, and further were willing to admit individual responsibility for future imports, but not universal collective responsibility. As Dr. Morse says, the war was ' not fought to uphold the trade in opium.' The war ' had been hanging in the air from the time of Lord Napier's protest.' ' It was only the beginning of a struggle, which lasted for twenty years, and which was to decide the national and commercial relations which were to exist between the East and the West.'

It may be added that the war never was between the English and Chinese people. The Chinese people were willing to trade and to live and let live throughout the country. It was a war of governments in which both were the

victims of untoward circumstances. Opium was
its accidental cause. Had the Manchus consented to have a British representative in Peking,
or even in Canton, and to treat him as something
less insignificant than a barbarian, the 'Opium
War' need never have occurred. It was a war
which put a stain on the name of Britain, a stain
which belonged at least equally to the other
nations, and most of all to the corrupt officials
of China, who from some of the highest officers in
the land to the lowest tidewaiters and smugglers
profited by and encouraged the vice. As the
American, John Quincey Adams, said, opium ' is
a mere incident to the dispute, but no more the
cause of the war than the throwing overboard the
tea in Boston harbour was the cause of the North
American revolution . . . the cause of the war
is the kotow '—that is, that the Manchu Emperor
should be acknowledged as lord of the world,
which is literally what he claimed to be.

Before the arrival of British forces, Commissioner Lin made several attempts against the
small British community. They were cannon-
aded, attacked by fire rafts, and in constant
danger, as well as in severe discomfort. Head
money and large rewards for the capture of ships
were offered by him.

On the arrival of British forces, numbering
16 ships of war mounting 540 guns, with 4000
men of all arms, Canton was blockaded on
June 28, 1840, Ningpo and the Yang-tze a month

later.   Then the Pei-ho was visited, where Kishen, the Manchu Viceroy, saw Capt. Elliot and arranged to have the whole question discussed and settled at Canton.   The British Pei-ho squadron accordingly returned to Canton.   In the meantime tropical disease was decimating the troops, and Britishers, shipwrecked on the coast, were shut up in cages $3\frac{1}{2} \times 3 \times 2$ ft. and exposed to the insults of the mob—an Englishwoman amongst them.

Capt. Elliot and Kishen both pursued a conciliatory policy ; but the naval withdrawal from the north had put the Manchu Government in heart again, so that Kishen was placed in serious difficulty, especially as he dared not yield to Elliot's demand for the cession of the then barren island of Hongkong as the British centre of trade. On January 7, 1841, the forts of Canton were again silenced and occupied, and an agreement finally entered into which gave Hongkong to the British.   Thereupon the British Government found Elliot's terms inadequate, recalled him and appointed Sir Henry Pottinger in his place ! If the British Government was dissatisfied with Elliot's inadequate terms, the Chinese Government was equally indignant with them, and ordered another High Commissioner to go to Canton and exterminate the foreign rebels.   War broke out again in February 1841.   By May Canton was being stormed by the British, when terms were again made, the troops withdrawn, and a report was sent to the Emperor that they had been thoroughly defeated, with consequent promotion and honours to the new Chinese Commissioner and his subordinates.

Sir Henry Pottinger was instructed, *inter alia*, as follows : ' The Chinese Government is fully entitled to prohibit the importation of opium, if it pleases, and British subjects who engage in a contraband trade must take the consequences of doing so '—an attitude similar to the present attitude towards American prohibition of liquor.

Sir Henry Pottinger promptly announced to the British merchants that national interests would no longer be subordinated to commercial interests, and that he aimed at compelling an honourable and lasting peace. Again the expedition set out for the north, took Amoy in August, Chusan in October, blockaded Ningpo, Chapu, Shanghai, Chinkiang (the strategic gate of the Yang-tze), and finally reached Nanking, which capitulated at once.

One of the discoveries made by the British forces was that the Manchu was a far braver foe than the Chinese. The Manchus fought to the death, or when defeated immolated both themselves and their families. A brave people, ruled over by an ignorant court, forbidden to trade, living as garrisons in the great provincial centres of China—one may properly regret the fall of enemies who deserved better arms, better leadership, and a better fate.

Finally the Treaty of Nanking was signed, August 29, 1842, on board H.M.S. *Cornwallis* by Sir Henry Pottinger and the High Commissioners Kiying and Ilipu, and ratifications exchanged next year. The Americans and French availed themselves of the British success and obtained similar treaties.

' Up to 1839 it was China,' says Morse, ' which dictated to the West the terms on which relations should be permitted to exist ; since 1860 it is the West which has imposed on China the conditions of their common intercourse : the intervening period of twenty years was one of friction, when the West had imposed its conditions, which China tried to minimise and resist.'

The Nanking treaty, which became the basis of later treaties, provided for perpetual peace and amity, the opening of Canton, Amoy, Foochow, Ningpo and Shanghai for residence and trade, with consular residence and right of direct communication with the Chinese mandarins, the cession of Hongkong, an indemnity for the opium (about half its value), trade debts and war expenses ; and the method of signature was prescribed ' so as to demonstrate clearly the absolute equality of England and China and of their sovereigns.'

The principal question not settled by the ' Opium War ' was the question of opium. In reply to Sir Henry Pottinger's suggestion for its better control by legalization, the Chinese plenipotentiaries declared that they dare not suggest

such a course to the Throne.   All honour to the
emperor, Tao Kuang, for his sincerity, if not for
his statesmanship !   Opium remained illegal and
contraband, British subjects dealing in it were
to receive no British protection, and at first it
was forbidden in Hongkong.   At the same time,
Sir Henry Pottinger warned the High Commissioners that the effect of imperial prohibition
would be to drive the trade into secret channels,
and that the British authorities could neither
police China nor enforce Chinese law on their own
subjects.   He also forbade the molestation of
British subjects for smuggling, but insisted that
the remedy must lie against the ship and cargo.
America, France and Russia admitted the ' contraband ' nature of the drug in their treaties.   In the
British treaty it received no mention.

As a matter of fact, the British Government did
not want, never had wanted, the opium trade.
The early importation of the drug was legitimate
as a medicine.   It was the Chinese themselves
who turned it into a ruinous vice, encouraged
thereto, despite the noble resistance of successive
Manchu rulers, by corrupt officials, chiefly Chinese.

X

THE TAIPING REBELLION AND THE 'ARROW' WAR

HOWEVER unfortunate may have been the foreign policy of the Emperor Tao Kuang, he had at least the merit of being an honourable and an able man. His son and successor Hsien-feng, 1851-1861, as M. Cordier indicates, ' had not a single quality to redeem his defects, too unintelligent to realize that the Manchu dynasty, foreign in a land which was hostile to it, was running towards destruction if the trend of its policy was not completely changed, profiting in no way from the lessons of the past, unconscious that the rebellions breaking out in his empire were only precursory signs of a storm which would sweep away his race, braving, despite the lesson of the Treaty of Nanking, the power of the " Western devils," who afresh were about to inflict on his country a profound humiliation, aiding by his conduct the discredit among his subjects of the Tartar princes, Hsien-feng let his ship wander according to the current of events, incapable of directing it through the channel, strewn with rocks, in which it sailed.'

The whole of his reign was darkened by the

swelling clouds of the Taiping or ' Great Peace ' Rebellion, whose supporters were called ' The Long-hair Rebels,' because they reverted to the top-knot of their forefathers and discarded the queue imposed by the Manchus two centuries before.

The Taiping Rebellion which, between 1851 and 1865, devastated the fairest half of China and was within an ace of shaking the Manchu from the throne, has association with our subject for several reasons. First, because in a sense it arose out of the sowing of Protestant Christian ideas in the land, as less directly did the more recent rebellion which finally overthrew the Manchu power. As to the Taiping Rebellion, it was primarily caused more by the Manchus than by the rebels, who were driven to resistance through danger. It resulted from the friction of persecution on the dynamic forces of Christianity in a raw state. From an excusable beginning the revolt degenerated into a welter of destruction— on both sides—but, in weakening the Manchu power, it also helped to bring China into the wider world. Gordon became famous as ' Chinese Gordon ' for his success against the rebels, and Sir Robert Hart as the chief of the Imperial Maritime Customs, which arose partly out of the disturbance.

The leaders who inspired the rebellions of 1851 and 1911—' a cycle of Cathay '—were both Cantonese and styled themselves Christians, Hung

Hsin-chuan and Sun Yat-sen. Hung was a Hakka, an emigrant tribe from Central China found in communities in the south. Son of the elder of his clan, he was also an able scholar; but, though high on the lists at the examinations, because he was a Hakka he was not given the coveted degree. During the examinations an American missionary, Issachar Roberts, rented and furnished a Chinese house in Canton, and invited candidates to stay with him. Hung and others accepted his invitation. Roberts had reading and prayer morning and evening, and the students, being interested in this novelty, attended. Hung and his intimate friends were impressed and took scriptures and tracts home, where they induced other scholars to join them in scripture study. The interest spread and the officials took alarm, thinking another anti-dynastic secret society was being formed. Hung and his friends were forbidden to meet. Later the Viceroy sent for him, to whom he told the truth, but who threatened armed suppression. As the meetings were continued, the Viceroy sent soldiers to fetch Hung and his friends, who thereupon ascended a hill, wrote in their own blood a statement giving the facts in regard to their religious meetings, and imploring religious liberty. The soldiers surrounded the hill, when a sudden impulse caused Hung and his company to rush down with a shout. The soldiers fled in a panic, throwing away their arms, and with these

discarded arms began the great rebellion. Hung
and his company started on' their northward
march to overthrow the Manchus, men and means
increasing daily, and his followers at first being
under strict discipline. They are said to have
marched nearly to Nanking without bloodshed or
pillage of any kind.

The above is the story as told to the Rev. James
Thomas by a reliable American, Dr. Yates, who
came into close contact with the leaders of the
Taipings. Another version is as follows :

Born in 1813, Hung began to sit at Canton for
the bachelor's degree in 1836. While there he
received a series of tracts written by Liang Ah Fa,
the first baptized Protestant convert, which tracts
he did not read, but no doubt scanned. Later he
fell into a violent fever, in the course of which he
received a religious ' revelation.' Six years are
said to have intervened between the receipt of
the tracts and his reading of them in 1843. They
confirmed the ' revelation ' he had received.
He baptized himself and his cousin. Others
joined them and they formed the Shang-Ti hui,
or Society of God. Preaching among the abori-
gines (Miao-tzǔ) of the neighbouring province,
Kuang Si, in 1844, they met with much success.
In 1846 Hung made the acquaintance of the Rev.
Isacchar Jacob Roberts of the American Board
of Foreign Missions, and asked for baptism, but
this was postponed. By 1849 his followers increased so as to disturb the official mind, especially

as members of the Triad Secret Society joined them. From a religious movement it became political, aiming at the overthrow of the Manchu Tartar dynasty. On September 25, 1851, Hung and his followers seized the town of Yung-nan and Hung was declared Emperor. The imperial government, impressed with the movement, now appointed Commissioner Lin of opium fame to suppress it. He died, and his successor failed to check Hung's advance.

By February 24, 1853, the rebels had obtained possession of the south of China, including most of the important towns on the Yang-tze River, and, on March 19, the great city of Nanking—or ' southern capital '—fell into their hands, when its large garrison of Manchus was slaughtered. For eleven years that city remained the rebel stronghold and capital. The rebel troops boldly attacked the north, of which better organization would have made them master. They actually crossed the Yellow River and almost reached Tientsin ; but the Manchu and Chinese imperial troops, under Sankolinsin, prevented entry to the capital and gradually drove them back to the Yang-tze. The terrible destruction wrought in the rich valley of the Yang-tze is generally attributed to the rebels, but it is doubtful if one side was less ruthless than the other.

Foreign powers were for long uncertain which side to support. In the Manchu Government they had always found a foe. In the rebels they had nominal friends. Had they early thrown in their lot with the rebels and organized the movement, history might have been changed; certainly the Manchu dynasty would have speedily fallen, and the moral tone of the movement probably been restored and strengthened.

Uncertainty produced neutrality, though foreign adventurers took part on both sides. By the time the Powers did face the question in order to make a final decision, Hung, who now styled himself in an imperial sense the brother of Christ, had become unbalanced by ‘ visions ’ and enervated by luxury. He and his followers had lost their high ideal and popular sentiment had turned against them. In consequence Britain and France, after beating the Manchus and wringing unwilling terms from them, decided to support the existing dynasty, in which they were then probably wise.

Nor was the Taiping Rebellion the only force that threatened the Manchu with extinction. In the western provinces there was a serious Moslem outbreak; in the north-east the Nien-fei, or ‘ Twisted Turbans,’ robbed and plundered; and along the coast the exasperated foreigner lowered and thundered. The Moslems, foreign by origin and followers of a foreign religion, were, in 1855, goaded into rebellion in the province of Yunnan, first by injustice on the part of local Chinese and then by an attempt in the following year to massacre them wholesale. Joined by the abori-

ginal tribes, the Moslems subdued the entire
Yunnan province and established their leader as
Sultan. But for the subsequent defection of his
two principal generals, there might have been a
great Moslem state ruling the west of China and
Central Asia. Despite these defections and internal disputes, the Moslem rebellion was only
crushed with difficulty after seventeen years of
strife, 1856-1873.

The Nien-fei, who broke out during the same
period, caused serious disturbance from Shantung
to Kansu. Sankolinsin, the Mongol commander,
known to the British sailors as 'Sam Collinson,'
whom we shall see as the chief military opponent
of the Franco-British forces in 1860, failed to
subdue them, and was killed in 1864 in an
encounter.

With Moslems and Nien-fei shaking their power
east and west, with the rich south lost to them,
and with the foundations sinking beneath their
throne, the Manchus were still arrogant enough
to drive England and France to declare war. The
so-called ' Opium War ' had not lowered their
disdain. Why should it ? Had they not justice
on their side ? What was the foreigner but a
manifestly immoral and uncultured barbarian ?
Yet the amazingly small force of foreigners
required to crush the very large Manchu and
Chinese forces might at least have opened any
but blind eyes to material facts. Perhaps the
smallness of these numbers even bolstered the

Manchu pride. It is remarkable that, at the time of the ' Opium War,' the total number of male foreign residents in China was only 259, of whom 147 were English. Even in 1859, when the ' Arrow War' was in progress, there were only 2148, of whom 1462 were in Hongkong, 127 in Canton, and 408 in Shanghai. Why then should the emperor of hundreds of millions pay any more attention to such paltry people than he would to a few buzzing flies ?

As in the ' Opium War,' so with the ' Arrow War' of 1858-60, the immediate *casus belli* was only the accidental, not the real cause. That cause was exactly the same as in the ' Opium War '—the attitude of overlordship to a vassal on the part of the Manchu Court and its representatives in Canton. Though, in accordance with the treaty, Shanghai and Ningpo had been opened in 1843 and Foochow and Amoy in 1844, Canton still remained closed. Every endeavour was officially made there to harass the foreigner. A Chinese who let a house to Dr. Hobson for medical treatment of Chinese was thrown into prison and kept there for six years. Vile placards were a common experience. In December 1842 the factories were burnt. Serious riots occurred in 1844 and 1846. In 1847 six young Englishmen went out for a walk and were never again seen alive. In this case the Manchu Viceroy, Ki-ying, administered prompt punishment and, in consequence of this just and wise action, was speedily

relieved of his office.   In the same year another
serious disturbance occurred at Fatshan near
Canton ; the British promptly seized the forts,
and later an agreement resulted for the opening
of Canton.   When the appointed time came for
such opening, the new Viceroy objected ; and
when the British Consul did not press the matter,
Canton became jubilant.   The Viceroy and his
subordinates were imperially rewarded for ' mana-
ging the barbarians.'   Viceroy and Governor
' dedicated to the principal temples votive in-
scriptions ascribing the victory to the merits and
patriotism of the people, and to those high officials
the grateful people of Canton presented honorific
tablets,' inscribed ' The People's Will is the City's
Strong Wall.'

This attitude at last aroused Lord Palmerston,
and in June 1850 he sent a stern note to Peking,
which was ' rejected with contumely.'   An imperial edict declared the sending of a letter to be
' contumacious and insulting in the extreme,' the
officials of the empire were to have ' no intercommunication with foreigners,' and they were
to send no reply to them, lest ' they should give
the slightest encouragement to their insolent
arrogance.'   The imperial edict praises the Canton
Viceroy Hsü for being ' thoroughly acquainted
with the diabolical schemes and manœuvres of
foreigners.'   Thus was the treaty of 1842 swept
aside.

Of course there was a measure of justification

for the court. To it the foreigner was manifestly a lawless barbarian. Had he not barbarously sold opium to China to the detriment of its people ? Though the imperial prohibition of opium at Canton had virtually opened every port on the coast to the trade, the court refused to realize its own responsibility and threw the entire blame on the wicked barbarian with his more powerful guns. And then there was that lamentable business, carried on chiefly by the Portuguese in Macao, of ' kidnapping ' coolies for Cuba, Peru, and California. Opium smuggling now carried on under foreign flags all along the coast, and coolie ' enslaving '—were not the foreigners manifestly barbarians ? How could one have intercourse with such degraded people ? Such was the court point of view, however incorrect. They saw only the mote in the barbarian's eye and ignored the beam in their own—the utter corruption of their officers. Moreover, they chose to despise the important trade in commodities other than opium, profitable as much to their own people as to the foreigner.

Unfortunately, there was still no foreign representative in the capital, nor any way of direct communication with the central authority. Moreover, intercourse between the various ports was rapidly increasing, chiefly through the advent of steamships, and the whole condition of European commerce and intercourse needed to be brought under a central control, unless smuggling, piracy, and all kinds of evils were to be encouraged by neglect.

Not only were the British oppressed in Canton, but in 1856 France was deeply stirred over the official execution in the neighbouring province of Kuangsi, after cruel torture, of the Abbé Chapdelaine and the persecution of the Chinese Christians there.

The British were finally moved to action over the lorcha *Arrow*, whence the war is commonly spoken of as the 'Arrow War.' A lorcha is a vessel with a foreign hull and Chinese rig. The *Arrow*, like many such boats, engaged, *inter alia*, in 'smuggling' opium, was licensed as a trading vessel by the Hongkong authorities. Under a British captain, with a Chinese crew, while flying the British flag, it was boarded in Canton, Oct. 18, 1856, by men of the Chinese navy; the British flag was hauled down, and, against the provisions of the 1842 treaty, the crew carried off as prisoners. The Commissioner Yeh would neither apologize nor send back the men, according to the terms of the treaty. He claimed that three of them were criminals, which may have been true. In brief, Canton was bombarded by the British, and the Chinese retaliated by setting fire to the British factories.

Britain and France, looking forward to peace after the Crimean War, were now reluctantly compelled to face the Chinese question. Lord Elgin was sent out by the British and Baron Gros

by the French, each with a fleet and men.   When
Lord Elgin reached Singapore he found urgent
letters from Lord Canning announcing the Indian
Mutiny, and appealing for aid.   With difficulty
Lord Elgin got into touch with the transports
and deviated them all to Calcutta, where they
were largely the means of saving the situation.
The crushing of the revolt in India brought an
end to the empire of the Grand Mogul and the
rule of the Mongol in Asia.

In China the plenipotentiaries Lord Elgin and
Baron Gros, with whom the American and Russian
representatives were in sympathy if not in arms,
endeavoured amicably to settle their difficulties
with the government, but soon discovered that
without coercive measures nothing would result.
Canton, which had been stormed a year before,
was taken on Jan. 5, 1858, and placed under a
Chinese governor acting in concert with a Franco-
British committee, and these kept the city in
order and prosperity for three years.   The Peking
governor sending an unsatisfactory answer to
the demands of the plenipotentiaries, the latter
sailed for the north and reached the Pei-ho, where
the forts were taken and the Treaty of Tientsin of
1858 signed.   This authorized the appointment
of ministers to Peking, also to London and Paris ;
eleven new ports were to be opened to trade, six
on the coast and five on the Yang-tze River ;
consuls were to be appointed ; foreigners were
to be permitted to travel in the interior, tariffs

to be revised, extra-territoriality and mixed courts of justice arranged, war expenses paid, the word ' barbarian ' no longer permitted in official documents, the Christian religion to be permitted, and so on. At that time there were about seventy Protestant missionaries in the country strictly confined to the few treaty ports. The Tientsin treaty now offered them freedom of movement. The United States and Russia secured treaties consequent on the Franco-British efforts.

In the following year 1859, when the British and French representatives endeavoured to reach Tientsin for the ratification of the treaties, they found their way barred, as (Sir) Robert Hart had already warned them would be the case. The Allies, attempting to remove the barriers from the Pei-ho, had to retire with severe loss, having failed to silence the positions at the mouth of the Pei-ho, now strongly fortified by Sankolinsin— ' Sam Collinson.' It was during the fighting there that the supposedly neutral American Capt. Tatnall uttered the historic phrase, ' Blood is thicker than water,' when he sent some of his men to help in towing boat-loads of marines for the rescue of the hard-pressed English admiral.

Lord Elgin and Baron Gros were again sent out to China. The British forces numbered 18,211, of whom 6894 were left to garrison Hongkong, Canton, the Chusan Islands and Shanghai. The French supplied 6300 men. A singular feature was the Cantonese Coolie Transport Corps of

2500 men, who rendered valuable service to the
Allies against their own government ! It was
during this period, also, that the curious situation
arose of the Shanghai officials naïvely appealing
to the foreign enemies of their government for
aid against the Taiping rebels. The Allies only
consented so far as the safety of Shanghai was
concerned.

This time the Taku forts were taken from the
rear, after a vigorous resistance. Tientsin was
reached August 25, 1860, and the Allied forces
pushed forward towards the capital, through a
difficult country swarming with Mongol, Manchu
and Chinese troops. During the advance, the
Manchus desiring a parley, Harry S. Parkes, Loch
and their party set out, and interviewed the
polite high Manchu officials; but after leaving
them, discovered that Sankolinsin had prepared
a formidable ambush for the Allied troops.
Sending on a warning to the Allies, Parkes
returned to interview the Manchu Commissioners,
later was seized by soldiers, thrown on his face
before Sankolinsin, he and his party loaded with
chains, carried off to Peking, and thrown into
jail. Several French officers and men suffered
a like fate, the Abbé de Luc being cruelly treated
and murdered.

The Allies pressed forward, despite anxiety as
to reserve ammunition, and took the Summer
Palace, a few miles from Peking. ' Nothing in
Europe can give any idea of such luxury,' wrote

General Montauban. He was unable to describe its splendour through ' bewilderment caused by the sight of such marvels.' It was thoroughly looted by the French and the small British cavalry contingent on the first day, and not least by the local Chinese.

Under threat of bombardment a gate of Peking was surrendered to the Allies, as also was Parkes with seventeen other living prisoners, and twelve of those who had been barbarously done to death. The sight of these determined the fate of the Summer Palace. Lord Elgin, despite the refusal to participate of the French—it had been built by French priests—gave it over to flames, or rather such part of it as remained after the fires started by Chinese looters. Lord Elgin's desire was to punish the court and spare the people.

The Tientsin treaties were revised and ratified, October 24 and 25, and early in November Peking was evacuated by the Allied troops. It may be noted here that General Ignatieff had been in Peking over a year, endeavouring to induce the Manchus to cede to Russia the territory east of the River Ussuri. In acknowledgment of his services as an intermediary with the Allies, he obtained the reward he had hitherto vainly sought.

The treaty confirmed that of Tientsin of 1858, the Emperor agreed to apologize, permanent legations in Peking were accorded, war indemnities increased, Tientsin opened as a port, Chinese emigration put under regulations, and Kowloon added to Hongkong. The French secured a similar treaty, and in addition full toleration of the Catholics. France's chief interest in China at that time was ecclesiastical. No matter what the attitude at home might be towards the Church, France was ever *fidei defensor* in China. The toleration of the Catholics included the return of mission property, which had been confiscated during the long period of persecution—a subject which resulted in considerable friction. ' To the *Chinese* but not to the French text . . . was added, surreptitiously as the Chinese Government had aways declared, the following clause : " And it shall be lawful for French missionaries in any of the provinces to lease or buy land and build houses." ' In 1903, America formally secured this right for all missions.

By the Treaty of Peking of 1860 were ended seventy years of diplomatic and warlike struggle. Until the termination of the East India Company's charter, relations were carried on between traders only, save for the unsuccessful Macartney and Amherst missions. The serious attempt made by Lord Napier to regulate trade and intercourse by means of responsible national representatives on terms of equality was thwarted by his death. The Manchu Court steadily refused any relation save that of an overlord to its vassal. The conscientious struggle of the Emperor against the opium evil on the one hand, and on the other the impossibility of Great Britain acting as China's coastguard to prevent the smuggling of a commodity so easily transported as opium, an enterprise in which men and ships of many nations were engaged, brought affairs to a crisis. The so-called 'Opium War' only opened the door somewhat wider to trade. It required the war of 1860 to destroy the foolish masquerade of haughty lordship over vassals, and to open the door to official relations on terms of equality. Not indeed until 1873 was the 'kotow' question finally settled when, on the coming of age of the Emperor T'ung Chih, the ambassadors of foreign nations were for the first time received in audience on terms of equality. The British Legation was established in Peking by the arrival on March 26, 1861, of the Hon. Frederick Bruce, but it was not till 1873 that the Chinese reciprocated by establishing a legation in London. Sir John Macleavy Brown, still the legal adviser to the Chinese Legation in London, entered Peking before missionaries were admitted within its walls.

Returning to the Taiping rebels, we find that by the accession of further forces they extended the area of their success through Kiangsu into the Chekiang province. Soochow, Hangchow and other cities fell into their hands. A force of foreign adventurers had been formed by Ward, an able American commander. With these, at first in the pay of a wealthy Shanghai banker, he fought the rebels. Later the force was disbanded

and Ward formed another force of Chinese called
' The Ever Victorious Army.' This foreign
armed, drilled and led corps was favoured and
adopted by the Chinese generals, of whom
Li Hung-Chang is the best known in the West.
When Ward was killed, Burgevine followed him,
but his overbearing manner brought about his
dismissal.   Later he went over to the rebels.   On
the recommendation of the British commander,
Captain Charles George Gordon was appointed.
He was then senior officer of the Engineers in
China, and had already led British contingents
in support of Ward.   Gordon marched from
success to success, and finally Soochow the great
rebel stronghold fell, where the ablest rebel leaders
held command.   It fell partly through internal
disputes among the rebels.   Gordon having promised and secured Li Hung-Chang's promise that
the eight rebel leaders and their men should be
granted their lives if they capitulated, was so
indignant next day, when Li Hung-Chang had
them shot, that he sought him with a gun but
failed to find him.   There may be some excuse
for Li's treachery, when one remembers that his
brother with his staff had been but recently
decoyed into a city by the rebels and all of them
massacred.   Gordon at once resigned his post,
and later refused the grant made him by the
emperor. The defection of Burgevine to the
rebels, and consideration of the importance of
putting a speedy end to the evils of the rebellion,

induced him to review his decision. He continued the struggle, rendering valuable service, till the fall of Nanking in 1864, when there came to an end a rebellion which had devastated the fairest provinces of China, destroyed its finest cities, and exterminated over twenty million of its people. Gordon's ' Ever Victorious Army,' which he recommended should become the nucleus of a standing army, was disbanded by Li Hung-Chang, lest it should become too powerful.

XI

THE CUSTOMS ; REBELLIONS ; WARS WITH
FRANCE AND JAPAN

ONE of the results of the Taiping Rebellion was the establishment of the Chinese Maritime Customs, which is to-day the main security for foreign loans to China, loans which have, alas! for the most part been squandered.

The actual founder of the Maritime Customs was Sir Rutherford Alcock, who secured the appointment in 1854 of (Sir) Thomas F. Wade, who was soon succeeded by Mr. Horatio Nelson Lay, a distant relative of the great Nelson, and with somewhat of his spirit. But the name of Sir Robert Hart will always be famous as the real maker of this remarkable service. It came into existence in Shanghai. The rebel attack on the native city drove the Chinese officials to safety in the small European settlement, which then, as now, was a 'city of refuge' because of its extra-territoriality. In the absence of any Chinese authority for the collection of customs duties from foreign vessels, a state of anarchy dangerous to present and future trade arose, and Sir Rutherford Alcock, the British Consul, was the means of solving the difficulty by an arrangement, the principle of which has remained in force ever since.   The service on its administrative side is under the sole control of a foreign (hitherto British) Inspector-General, who engages the staff, collects all dues, and, after paying expenses and sums chargeable upon mortgage of the revenue, pays the balance to his Chinese colleague to be dealt with as the latter's government may direct, and has no further responsibility for its expenditure.

To deal in detail with the Lay-Osborn difficulty which led to Lay's retirement from the Chinese service is unnecessary.   Suffice it that, wounded in Shanghai and home on leave, he was instructed by Prince Kung to purchase a fleet of armed ships and engage crews, for the purpose of ending the Taiping Rebellion.   A misunderstanding arose. The fleet was bought and brought to China by Capt. Sherard Osborn and a British complement, but Mr. Lay objected to entire Chinese control over it.   The Chinese Government, perhaps naturally, demurred; dismissed him on generous terms; and the British Government sold the fleet to save it from getting into objectionable hands.   Robert Hart took Lay's place and made the customs the only honest service the Chinese Government had or has, unless we except the other services which have grown out of it.   He became China's wisest adviser, and if only the government had possessed a modicum of statesmanship, China might have

outrivalled Japan in progress. The present
national university arose out of the college he
founded. He ' induced the sending abroad of the
first diplomatic mission ; lighted the coast with
lighthouses and lightships ; founded the modern
and efficient postal and telegraph service ;
arranged terms after the Franco-Chinese War ' ;
and ' had something to do with every important
matter in foreign and Chinese intercourse during
forty years.' Appointed British Minister in 1885,
his sense of duty compelled him to deny himself
that honour and to remain at his old post. He
resigned in 1907, and died in England in 1911.
His successor, Sir Francis Aglen, has well maintained the honour of the service.

In 1862 another Moslem rising broke out in
Kansu and Shensi, which was quelled between
1868-1874 by General Tso Tsung-t'ang, Kansu's
fifteen million inhabitants being reduced, it is
said, to one million. It was followed by the
Yakoob Beg rising in Kashgaria, when Tso
between 1874-8, with his Agricultural Army,
which provisioned itself by sowing and reaping,
quelled the Moslems without wasting such a rare
commodity as mercy on the conquered.

The ' Tientsin massacre ' of 1870 showed mob
hatred, generally spurred by the *literati*, at its
worst. It was a time of epidemic ; children died
in numbers, including many in the Catholic
orphanage ; vile rumours was spread of kidnapping, the taking out of eyes and internal

organs for foreign medicine, etc. The French Consul acted somewhat indiscreetly, and the mob burnt the orphanage and cathedral, massacred the sisters, several priests and the Consul. ·

The Loochoo Islands were Chinese, but when Japanese sailors residing there visited Formosa and were murdered by aboriginal head-hunters, Japan in 1868 invaded Formosa. Sir Thomas Wade, the British Minister, acted as intermediary and induced China to compensate Japan. By some slip in the terms of settlement, Japan was later able to claim the Loochoo Islands, and China had reluctantly to yield.

In 1875 the Emperor T'ung Chih ' became a guest on high ' through the medium of smallpox. His mother, the celebrated Empress Dowager Tze-Hsi, who had put him on the throne, and virtually ruled during the thirteen years of his reign, now replaced him with another child, thus enabling her to continue her hold of the reins of power.

The reign of Kuang Hsü is remarkable for the advance of Western ideas, unwisely resisted as long as possible by the government, and the rapid increase of foreign influence. The Japanese sought Western knowledge and became enlightened as well as powerful. The Chinese waited for it to be thrust on them and became weaker year by year.

In 1874 the British Consul Margary was ambushed and killed at Manwyne on the borders of

Burma, where he saved the lives of the British expedition by the sacrifice of his own. In the negotiations which followed five new trading ports were opened, as well as six ports of call on the Yang-tze.

In 1876 the Chinese at last condescended to favour the Court of St. James's with a Minister, Kuo Sung Tao.

In 1871, during the Yakoob Beg rising, Russia had availed itself of the opportunity of taking 'temporary possession' of Kuldja, but later declined to restore it to China. Ch'ung Hou, the only Manchu of high rank who had ever been sent abroad—he had been to France to apologize for the Tientsin massacre—went to Russia, and negotiated the Treaty of Livadia by which the best part of Ili was ceded to the Russians. China repudiated the arrangement, and Ch'ung Hou would have lost his head but for an earnest appeal from Queen Victoria. War with Russia being imminent, General Gordon was called in. He pointed out the unfitness of China for such a war and advised negotiation. Marquis Tseng was sent to Russia, and Ili was bought back for nine million roubles.

In 1877 the province of Shansi was devastated by a terrible famine, when upwards of nine million people perished. Missionaries took an active part in famine relief, Timothy Richard and David Hill being the best known. Thus was laid the foundation stone of modern famine relief in

China. From this date Timothy Richard began his life's great work of urging education upon the government. If it were Christian work to relieve famine, it was more so to prevent it, and he saw that this could only be done through education, with consequent development of the fine natural resources and of improved communications. In the preceding year, 1876, a British firm had built the first railway in China, 14 miles long, from Shanghai to Woosung at the mouth of the river. By order of the Empress Dowager it was bought, torn up and thrown away in Formosa, and this during the time that the famine was devastating Shansi, devastating it because food, plentiful in other provinces, could not be transported to the starving people.

France went to war with China in 1884. Since 1715 the French had been interested in Annam. Early in the eighteenth century French priests had been successful there in enthroning a king. His death caused the death of many of the priests and thousands of their converts. In 1858 France extended its power over Annam and Tonking. China naturally resented this interference with its vassal, and both sympathized with and aided the native rulers in their long-continued resistance. In 1884 fighting occurred between French and Chinese troops. The Viceroy Li Hung-Chang urged negotiations and made terms, China agreeing to withdraw from Tonking. Li understood that by these terms the Chinese troops had three months' time in which to withdraw, Fournier understood it was three weeks. In three weeks the French attacked in Tonking and were severely repulsed, whereupon Admiral Courbet, repulsed also from Formosa, steamed across to Foochow. There, on the ground that war had not been formally declared, he entered the river unopposed by the forts, and within seven minutes of the commencement of his attack, strewed it with the utterly unprepared Chinese vessels, filling it with wreckage and drowning sailors. Sir Robert Hart arranged terms almost identical with those previously made between Li and Fournier.

In 1891 the Yang-tze ports were in peril, as also foreigners throughout the land, through false and vile reports published by a noted Chinese scholar (Chou Han). The ' stupid people ' were incited to destroy mission and other property, which they cheerfully did, harrying the defenceless foreigners, and in the end receiving a measure of punishment, from all of which the real culprit, the scholar Chou Han, of course escaped.

Korea now became a centre of further humiliation to China—the bitterest humiliation she had ever had. In 1894 the Japanese, the ' dwarfs ' she so much despised, in sharp stern conflict revealed the Chinese Government for what it really was, a government of blind and deaf conservatives.

Korea, vassal of China, had been the intermittent battle-ground between China and Japan for a thousand years.   In 1875 the trouble began again, and ten years later—thanks to quarrels between Korean progressives and conservatives—China and Japan became further involved.   Terms were then arranged, according to which China and Japan withdrew their troops and both nations agreed not to send forces into Korea without previous notification each to the other. In the meantime Russia made a pretext of the disturbed condition of Korea to move troops to its borders, and Britain countered by taking charge of Port Hamilton, which it restored to China in 1887 when the trouble was over.

By 1894 Li Hung-Chang had raised a foreign armed and drilled army, a navy had been trained and disciplined by a British officer, Captain Lang, and the coast fortified.   Arms may be bought, but spiritual forces are not marketable.   Corruption bred incompetence.   For instance, the Admiralty was made an appendage to the Board of Works which was rebuilding the Summer Palace —destroyed by Lord Elgin—for the Empress Dowager, and the navy funds were sunk in that palace.

In 1894 a revolt in Korea drove the king to appeal to China for aid.   The Chinese sent 2000 men before announcing the fact to Japan— a technical breach of the treaty very welcome to that country.   Already well acquainted with everything that went on in China, the Japanese despatched 10,000 men to Korea, sank the transport *Kowshing*, which was steaming under British officers and flying the British flag. The Chinese army was hopelessly beaten and, despite a brave fight, the Chinese fleet was forced to surrender in Wei-hai-wei harbour. By the Treaty of Shimonoseki of 1895, Korea was declared independent—soon after to fall into the hands of the Japanese—the Liao-Tung Peninsula, including the impregnable position of Port Arthur, the splendid island of Formosa, and the Pescadores were ceded to Japan and four more Chinese ports opened.

Russia intervened, as did Germany and France, and Japan in exchange for thirty million taels was deprived of Liao-Tung and Port Arthur. For its intermediary services, Russia received permission to carry the Trans-Siberian Railway across Manchuria to Vladivostok, and to build a railway through Manchuria to Dalny near Port Arthur. Thus were the seeds sown by Russia of the Russo-Japanese war ten years later.

In 1897 two German Catholic missionaries were murdered. Germany, hailing the opportunity of definitely challenging France's erstwhile protectorate over Catholic missionaries, landed a force at Tsing-tao, and demanded an indemnity, railway and mining concessions in the province of Shantung, the cashiering of the provincial governor and a 99 years' lease of Kiao-chow—terms which hardly increased Chinese love of missions ! Russia now pressed for and obtained the magni-

ficent harbour and fortress of Port Arthur ; the
French Kuangchow Bay ; even the Italians, with
nominal interests, wanted Sanmen Bay, but at
last the unhappy worm turned and snapped a
refusal. Britain, as much in the interests of
China as her own, took over the naval centre,
Wei-hai-wei. Concession-hunters flocked to
Peking, and it seemed as if the melon were indeed
about to be divided. At the end of 1897 the first
stormy mutterings of the Boxer uprising were
heard.

The outstanding feature of the Manchu dynasty
during the latter half of its existence was its grudg-
ing foreign policy. Its second noble emperor,
K'ang-hsi, was of generous mind and would have
been of uniformly generous action, but for the
ominous doings of aggressive traders and of
quarrelsome ecclesiastics. The reaction which
occurred under his son Yung-Cheng was natural,
and from his reign, 1723, for over a hundred years
China was almost a closed country. Given the
then existing type of trader, Chinese equally with
foreign, and the oppressive, indeed vicious method
in which trade and intercourse were conducted, it
cannot be said that there was any hope of reform.
Force is generally an unwholesome remedy. When
it is a remedy it leaves behind scars hard to
heal. Whether other means than 'iron tube and
reeking shard' would have been effective, who
shall say ? The men were such, the situation was
such that wise and generous Western statesmen

saw no way but force, and conscientious and patriotic Chinese statesmen no way but resistance. Force was used. It was effective. It left scars. We are still busy trying to heal them, and some people quite clearly prefer them open and unhealed.

As I have written elsewhere, ' while there were excellent men among the British merchants, no evidence is necessary to show the conditions which naturally prevailed in a seaport where the horny-handed of many nations assembled,' where shore-leave placed before them the temptation of vile spirits served by Chinese who robbed them when drunk. A hundred sailors died at Canton during every half-yearly shipping season. Those were the days before mission hospitals, mission schools and colleges, famine relief and a host of other gracious deeds had shown to the Chinese that Occidentals were not such utter barbarians, nor such grotesque creatures, as outward appearance might suggest. Had the earlier trading relations of West with East been conducted in a spirit of mutual welfare, instead of with the manners of the buccaneer, had the Gospel been preached in a more Christian and less dogmatic spirit, the East might have welcomed the West. But, for the proper cultivation of ' Christian charity ' on the one hand and of Confucian ' kindness to men from afar ' on the other, hard blows were deemed necessary by both sides.

XII

REFORM

BLOW had succeded blow before China awakened
to a realization of its perilous condition. The
'Opium War,' the 'Arrow War,' the Taiping
Rebellion, the French War, had only dazed the
government. It still remained covertly, and
often overtly, as anti-foreign as before. The
foreigner and his mechanical inventions and
power were still barbarian, even though that
term was perforce excluded from official documents.

But to be defeated by the Japanese, a race of
pirates, a race despised, that was indeed a rousing
blow, and not to the government only, but to
the thoughtful classes throughout the country—
and, indeed, to foreign nations also. China, the
giant nation of the world, had proved to be the
feeblest. Its utter weakness was revealed to the
world. The nations seized their opportunity.
The eagles gathered to the prey. The 'sphere of
influence' period arrived. Bargains were driven
as to who should influence, where. Russia
claimed Manchuria as its 'sphere of influence,'
which irritated Japan; Germany the province of

Shantung, with an eye to all northern China ;
France the southern borders and Yunnan ; Japan
the province of Fukien ; Great Britain the
Yang-tze Valley. It seemed indeed as if
the Chinese surmised correctly, that the melon
was already being divided amongst the foreign
powers.

In 1896 and 1897 occurred attacks on guiltless
Protestant missionaries, who indeed were as
distressed as the Chinese over the ills of China.
As already mentioned, in 1897 two Roman
Catholic missionaries were murdered by robbers
in a small out-of-the-way village in the S.W. corner
of Shantung. The robbers also looted the village,
and the affair was in no sense anti-foreign. But
Germany had for months been examining the
coast and had already informed Russia, Austria
and Italy of its intention to acquire a naval base
in China. With this object in view its gunboats
had been visiting the coasts of Fukien, Chekiang
and Shantung. The two murdered missionaries
were Germans. Thirteen days after the catastrophe and only four days after the news became
known, Germany seized the island of Tsing-tao.
Until 1890 France had been the recognized protector of Catholic missions. Then Germany
claimed its rights over Germans, and here was
the first effective opportunity for asserting these
rights. Germany, as shown, demanded the
cashiering of the governor, indemnities, the port
of Kiao-chow adjoining Tsing-tao, and sole rail-

way and mining rights in the province of Shantung.

Chinese hesitation to grant the demands gave the Kaiser his opportunity for declaring the German navy inadequate and for introducing his naval bill—thus do events in China have repercussion in the West. Reinforcements were sent out under Admiral Prince Henry of Prussia. Then it was that the Kaiser spoke with swelling words against a helpless foe :

'I am conscious that it is my duty to extend and enlarge what my predecessors have bequeathed me. . . . May everyone in those distant regions be aware that the German Michael has firmly planted his shield, with the device of the German eagle, upon the soil of China, in order once for all to give his protection to all who ask for it. . . . Should anyone essay to detract from our just rights or to injure us, then up and at him with your mailed fist.'

This is quite as haughty as the Chinese edicts up to the sixties. Admiral Prince Heinrich rose to the occasion :

'Most august emperor : most mighty king and lord, illustrious brother . . . of one thing I may assure your Majesty, neither fame nor laurels have charm for me. One thing is the aim that draws me on, it is to declare in foreign lands the gospel of your Majesty's hallowed person, to preach it to everyone who will hear it, and also to those who will not hear it. . . . Let the cry resound far over the world, most august, most mighty, beloved emperor, king and lord for ever and ever.'

Such was the ' gospel ' Germany sent to China to avenge the murder by outlaws of two of her Christian missionaries, who would have been the first to cry, ' Father, forgive them, for they know not what they do.' Which was the greater ' outlaw,' the brigand or the Kaiser, history has already told.

The treaty of March 6. 1898, as a matter of course granted all the Kaiser's demands. ' We must find in the manner in which the Kiao-chow affair was conducted, not the sole cause, but the chief cause of the Boxer movement and the support given to it by the Empress Dowager.' So, very truly, speaks M. Cordier. He might have added that before the Boxer movement it was the chief cause in the rise of the reform movement.

Within a week of the German seizure of Tsing-tao, Russia, anxious for the whole of the north as its sphere and disappointed at not securing Kiao-chow as its intended ice-free port, availed itself of permission granted in a previous covenant to anchor its warships for the winter in Port Arthur. In further conventions of March 27 and May 7, 1898, Russia obtained a 25 years' lease of this almost impregnable naval fortress and of Ta-lien-wan, with the adjacent waters, islands and peninsulas, also a zone of 60 miles

prohibited to the entry of Chinese soldiers. Port
Arthur was to be a great naval station ; Ta-lien-
wan, or Dalny, a trading port. Rights were also
obtained to connect Harbin and Vladivostok by
rail. China evacuated Port Arthur, March 27,
1898.

France obtained the Bay of Kuang-chow-wan
in the south for 99 years as a naval station,
with its dependencies and mainland, and entered
into possession April 22, 1898. China at first
refused to ratify, but yielded, on January 5,
1900, after the murder of two French naval
officers on November 12, 1899, and concessions
for railway building were also granted.

Britain, whose policy had always aimed at
equality of opportunity for trade, and who had
no desire to see the break-up of China, or for
territorial expansion, had stood alone in protesting against the closing of Port Arthur. Its
protest was in vain, for Germany and France
were accomplices of Russia. Every British endeavour made for the maintenance of China's
integrity was thwarted, especially by Russia.
China in despair now secretly offered Wei-hai-wei
to the British. Lord Salisbury replied that
British policy sought ' to discourage the alienation
of Chinese territory,' but he afterwards consented
to occupy Wei-hai-wei immediately on Japan's
prospective withdrawal, in which step Japan
concurred. Wei-hai-wei was leased to Great
Britain ' for so long a period as Port Arthur shall

remain in the occupation of Russia.' Britain did not re-fortify Wei-hai-wei, but maintained it as a naval health station. On June 9, 1898, Britain, anxious about its defences of Hong-kong, was granted the whole of the Kowloon peninsula on a lease of 99 years, thus increasing the territory of Hongkong from 29 to 405 square miles.

After the treaties of alienation came the 'non-alienation declarations,' by which China engaged not to alienate certain territories to other powers. France first sought and obtained such a declaration on March 15, 1897, in regard to the large island of Hainan. Britain followed in regard to the Yang-tze Valley, February 11, 1898 ; France again concerning the provinces bordering on Tonking, April 10, 1898 ; Japan in regard to the province of Fukien opposite its new Formosa possession, April 26. British action in regard to the Yang-tze Valley was 'an asser-tion of the open door' to all the powers equally. Germany claimed the open door everywhere else, but denied it to others in Shantung, and its claim prevailed. In 1899 Britain and Russia agreed that Russia would not interfere in the Yang-tze basin, and Britain would not interfere beyond the Great Wall.

Following all this came the demand for ' Treaty Port concessions,' or enlargements—Russia in Newchwang ; Germany in Tientsin ; Japan in Amoy and Foochow ; France, Russia, Germany,

Japan, Belgium in Hankow; French, British and American in Shanghai.

In 1899, as already stated, even Italy, with few interests in the East, sought a naval base at Sanmen Bay, off the Chekiang coast. England, Germany, France agreed to support Italy in a friendly way. The Italian Minister unwisely demanded it with an ultimatum, and was in consequence recalled by Italy for exceeding his instructions. His recall gave courage to the Chinese Government. Italy withdrew its claim, and China exulted as over a victory.

As Dr. Morse says : ' No country with a tithe of its area and population had ever been subjected to such a series of humiliations, or to so many proofs of the low esteem in which it was held . . . and no country had so thoroughly deserved its fate ; no country had ever shown itself so incapable of correcting admitted abuses in its administration, or of organizing the resources of an exceedingly rich country, inhabited by a sturdy race with many good qualities.' No wonder thoughtful Chinese had long been indignant and looked for a way to avoid the partition of their land.

Long before the humiliation of the Japanese war, the crying need for internal reform had been urged upon the official and educated classes by Dr. Young J. Allen, an American Methodist missionary, and Dr. Timothy Richard, an English Baptist, heads of the S.D.K. (Society for the

Diffusion of Christian and General Knowledge among the Chinese ; a title manifestly of Scottish origination, later shortened to The Chinese Christian Literature Society). During and after the Japanese war Dr. Allen boldly published correct news, declared the facts and showed the perilous condition of China. With the faithfulness of a true friend, he depicted the folly of the government and people in their persistent conservatism, contrasting their unwillingness to learn with the fortunate willingness of the Japanese. Dr. Richard, of famine relief fame, who had already gained the attention of such Viceroys as Li Hung-Chang and Chang Chih-tung, was writing inspiring articles and publishing enlightening books exposing China to the Chinese in the light of its own and of world history. Others were also translating books from the Japanese on modern development.

More than to any others was it due to these two men that the Chinese were led to see a way of escape from their peril. Their publications were read throughout the length and breadth of the land. ' From the Emperor on his throne to the village scholar on his hard stool,' they were awaited with an astonishing eagerness to which I can personally testify.

It was early in 1898 that the reform movement found its leader. Again it was a Cantonese who came to the front ; this time not as an anti-dynastic revolutionary, but as one who would save the dynasty and China. The three Cantonese who in the nineteenth century sought to reform China were, first, Hung Hsin-chuan, who with his Taiping rebels devastated half the land, and was only crushed by foreign aid. The second, Sun Yat-sen, anti-dynastic and republican, the son of a Chinese Christian, was educated in a mission school, and became the first graduate under Sir James Cantlie of the Hongkong School of Medicine, now part of the Hongkong University. In 1895 he and others planned and carried out an armed attack on Canton. It failed, and he fled for and found a refuge among his fellow-countrymen overseas, though a price was on his head that would have made many of them rich. He is described as of 'transparent honesty,' 'manifest patriotism,' 'simplicity of character,' 'readiness to endure all for his country's sake.' As a destroyer he has had few equals; constructive powers were not his.

The third reformer was K'ang Yu-wei, who, if he had been a practical statesman, might have become the Mazzini of the reform movement. A fine scholar, after reading with avidity all the publications of Dr. Allen, Dr. Richard, and of their society, as also numerous translations of universal history chiefly from the Japanese, he presented his case for reform with such ability that he earned for himself the title of ' The modern Sage ' of China. It must never be thought that reformers were lovers of the foreigner. Far

from that being the case, foreign hatred—more
of nations than of individuals—was their powerful
stimulant. It was unnecessary and unwise, if
not surprising. So K'ang for long detested and
despised the barbarian, till on leaving his ancestral
home he came into contact in Hongkong and
Shanghai with a civilization which astounded
him.

In the spring of 1898 he found himself in
Peking, where his writings had become influential.
All the younger and many of the older mandarins
and scholars, Chinese and Manchu, felt the need
of reform. Like K'ang Yu-wei they were not
anti-dynastic, but sought to convert both court
and government to the reform and reorganization
of the empire. In this K'ang and his reform
party soon had promise of success. With less
haste they would have made more speed. Perhaps
some haste was excusable, for China had lost
much time, was far away behind Japan, and
events were pressing. One need have little hesitation in saying that had the reform party been
more moderate it would have established reform,
and thus have saved Boxer risings, Sun Yat-sens,
revolutions, perhaps even the Russo-Japanese
war—fought on Chinese soil—withal the Manchu
throne and who knows what else? Haste was
its undoing.

Having formed his plans for reform on the
basis of the publications of Richard and Allen,
K'ang went to Peking to advocate their adoption.

The ideas, not the haste, were theirs. Sponsored by high provincial authorities, including Yuan Shih-k'ai, and supported by the Prime Minister, Weng T'ung-ho, he was in 1898 introduced to the Emperor Kuang Hsü, who became his eager supporter. The Emperor's interest had first been awakened to the wisdom of the West, in 1894, by the beautifully printed and bound Bible presented to the Empress Dowager on her sixtieth birthday by ten thousand Christian women of China. Now, he proceeded to read K'ang's *Reform of Russia* by Peter the Great, and his *Reform of Japan*. He also read the weekly reform paper, which was largely copied from the S.D.K. magazine. The Reform Society and paper were supported by official funds. Some of the leading statesmen and provincial rulers were amongst its members as well as all the ablest young scholars. The Emperor was urgent to carry out their scheme of reform. Despite a measure of temporarily successful opposition from conservative elements, the times and the scholars and officials of the country were ripe. This is easily revealed by the eagerness displayed five years later, when official opposition was removed.

During the Hundred Days of Reform, edict followed edict. A complete change in the system of examinations was ordered. No longer were the hoary classics to be considered sufficient training for the rulers of the nation. Ancient and modern history, national and foreign, were to be studied; also political systems, mathematics, arts and sciences. The government was to be completely organized on modern practical lines, which of course was not pleasant news to the horde of barnacles and limpets so firmly attached to the waterlogged ship of state. An educational system after the most approved Western fashion was to be established. Temples were to be turned into schoolrooms and colleges to be built, equipped and staffed immediately.

XIII

REACTION

IN 1898 the Chinese millenium seemed to have dawned. Sir Robert Hart called me into his room at Pei-tai-ho, and with beaming face read one of these edicts. ' I never expected to live to see this,' he said. Alas ! there had been undue haste. Decrees which should have been spread over years were rushed forth in three brief months. They were revolutionary in character rather than reformatory. The Empress Dowager may be likened to a spider on the alert, weaving her web to catch the reforming Emperor and the K'ang Yu-wei's. But this would be an unfair illustration. She was watching, it is true, watching with interest, with mingled feelings, perhaps with a half-open mind. If she distrusted a Cantonese one cannot wonder. At any rate she was always ready for emergencies. In reality it was the reformers who spun a web and it blew round themselves. They spun it for her because they knew her power and were afraid of it. Against the urgent advice of Dr. Richard, who believed she could be converted, they recommended to the willing Emperor—who had no love for her—that she should be confined, lest the old schemer should spoil their plans.

The Emperor called in Yuan Shih-k'ai, himself a reformer, who, despite his denial, is believed by many to have promised to execute the Viceroy Jung-lu, the Dowager's henchman, and then confine the Dowager in her palace. If that story be true, then Yuan's word was as much as his bond to the Emperor, as it was later to the republic which he was later to forswear. But, after all, Jung-lu was his sworn ' blood-brother ' and patron. How could he be expected to kill him ? Instead of relieving him of his office and his life, he seems to have told him the whole plot. That was before noon of July 20. At any rate Jung-lu hastened to the Dowager, reached her in the Summer Palace by 5 p.m., and was back in Tientsin the same night to lead his troops to support her against the Emperor and his reformers.

The same night she took steps for the Emperor's deposition, swooped down on the capital, seized and imprisoned him, executed seven of the ablest young leaders of the Reform Club, and dismissed or degraded reforming officials whole-sale. One of her keenest desires was to seize the arch-conspirator K'ang Yu-wei. For this purpose she stopped all trains on the 22nd. But K'ang had escaped.

On the 17th, the Emperor, anxious about his own impending fate, had decreed that K'ang should set out immediately for Shanghai to start a reform newspaper there. He also sent him a private note saying: 'You must get away at once and devise means to save me without delay.' K'ang hid himself in Peking for two days and only left on the 20th. Reaching Tientsin and not realizing his danger he boarded a Chinese steamer. Not liking it he changed over to a British steamer, and actually went ashore for a walk during its stay in Chefoo, unaware that orders had arrived in code for his arrest and execution. Happily for him the official was away and had taken the secret code with him. Outside Shanghai, K'ang's ship was met by a British Consul and, to save an international affair through arrest in Shanghai, he was offered a passage to Hongkong on a British vessel. His life was saved—but he was doomed to exile, and to learn of the bitter extermination of his kinsmen, the destruction of his ancestral graves, and to live under the anxious load of a great price upon his head.

The Empress Dowager, having swept away most of the reforms and reformers, restored the sinecure yamens and officials of Peking. She permitted the founding on modern lines of a university in Peking and of secondary schools in provincial capitals, but left all provincial education to voluntary effort and restored the temples to their owners. The old style examinations were also reinstated, and the Manchus were again armed with bows and matchlocks.

Outbreaks against foreigners naturally followed in various places. Even in the capital foreigners were attacked by the fierce troops of the rough Kansu general, Tung Fu-hsiang, which had been specially brought in to overawe reform. The apparent ' cowing ' of Italy over Sanmen Bay encouraged the anti-foreign spirit. Every province in the empire took its turn in foreigner-baiting. In Manchuria there was bitterness against the Russians for shooting down innocent peasants. In Shantung the feeling against Germans was even more bitter ; for the Germans took the law into their own hands without respect to China's sovereignty. The government made a covert demonstration against the Germans by marching 22,000 Chinese troops into Shantung, nominally for ' manœuvres.' Hostility to foreigners was thereby increased in Shantung as well as to everyone connected with foreigners, chiefly Chinese converts. Later, everything foreign became an object of hatred, for an old society was revived, formerly anti-dynastic, but whose hatred was cleverly transferred against the foreigner. This was the so-called Boxer Society, whose real name may be translated ' Fists for Justice and Peace.'

The Boxers began their assault by murdering the Rev. S. M. W. Brooks of the Church Missionary Society on December 30, 1899. The Governor of the province, the infamous Manchu, Yü Hsien, was removed from Shantung to Shansi.

On the way he easily persuaded Prince Tuan, father of the recently appointed heir-apparent, to support the Boxers, whom he believed, as did the rest of the infatuated people, to possess magical powers of resistance to foreign bullets. The provinces of Shantung and Chihli began to swarm with Boxers. Outrage after outrage took place. The north was unsafe for travel. The whole country became affected. The Empress Dowager —against the advice of her favourite adviser, the Viceroy Jung-lu—let the campaign have free course, and Boxer drill began to be carried on even in the palace grounds.

On June 10 the foreign legations in Peking were in such peril that Admiral Seymour left Tientsin with 1800 men for their relief. On the 24th, when only 25 miles distant, he was compelled to fight his way back with considerable loss. On the 11th the Japanese Chancellor of Legation was murdered. On the 13th began the destruction of outlying legations and missions, whereupon the British Legation and the Roman Catholic Pei-tang Cathedral became the centres of refuge. On the 20th, the German Baron von Ketteler was shot by a Manchu sergeant. On the 23rd Professor Huberty James was tortured and beheaded.

Now began the siege of the Legation and the Cathedral. Both would have fallen, but for the feigned obedience and deliberate inaction of the Viceroy Jung-lu. After two months of severe sufferings, on August 14 the British Legation with its 873 foreigners and 3100 Chinese, and the Cathedral with its handful of foreigners and three to four thousand Chinese, were relieved by the Allied forces. In the meantime thousands of Christian converts had been massacred, nor had the common people failed to suffer severely at the hands of the ravaging Boxers and the unrestrained soldiers.

There were high Chinese officials who stood out bravely against this mad orgy. For instance, to the Yang-tze Viceroys it is due that the greater part of China was kept in order ; to Tuan Fang, Governor of Shensi, and to the Governor of Szechwan, that the missionaries there escaped. When the Dowager sent off her telegrams to all viceroys and governors to exterminate the foreigners, two ministers of state dared to alter the word ' exterminate ' to ' protect ' in certain of them. They paid the price, as they expected, with their heads.

The Empress Dowager fled, taking with her the Emperor, first to T'ai-yuan-fu, then further west to Hsi-an-fu, 1000 miles from Peking. Sixteen months later, by invitation of the foreign Powers, she returned, to find her buried treasure intact, to which she now added the immense spoil she brought with her from the provinces. By this time terms had been arranged and peace declared.

The Boxer troubles had, not without reason, enabled Russia to strengthen its position in

Manchuria. The Blagovestchensk massacre horribly stained its name, when 5000 Chinese men, women and children were driven into the waters of the Amur and perished. Korea, too, presented itself as a field for Russian exploitation; but the advance of the northern Colossus brought protests from both Japan and Britain. In 1903 the Trans-Siberian railway was carried to Port Arthur, menacing Japan in general and its interests in Korea in particular. Japan demanded the military evacuation by Russia of Manchuria and recognition of Japan's suzerainty over Korea. Russia's delay in negotiations stirred Japan to break off relations; and, on Feb. 8, 1904, war broke out, which raised the prestige of Japan and lowered that of Europe throughout all Asia.

Russia lost her Far Eastern Fleet; the Russian Grand Fleet also, with 14,000 men, was buried beneath the Japan Sea by Admiral Togo. The Russian army, ill found and worse led, was gradually driven northward along the line of their railway, fighting bravely, but in vain, against a sober army not led by ignorant, corrupt and inebriated officers. The Portsmouth Treaty was made, through the influence of President Roosevelt, by which Korea came under Japanese suzerainty, the rights of Russia in Port Arthur and its peninsula were ceded to Japan. also the southern half of the great island of Saghalien, as well as other matters.

And this war took place on Chinese territory. The much-dreaded Colossus was broken by the ' pigmies ' of Japan. Could China hold up her head again ? Her only hope now was to follow Japan's example. This became clear even to the Empress Dowager and the Manchu backwoodsmen. Reform again became the order of the day. The battering blows of sixty years had at last aroused the sleeper—too late for the dynasty but not for the race. In 1905-6 orders were given that the administration was to be revised, the examination and educational system changed, the Manchu garrisons disbanded, the army and navy reorganized, railways extended, opium suppressed, and the criminal law revised with the abolition of torture. Influential missions were sent abroad to study systems of constitutional government, and in 1906 local and provincial parliaments were ordered to be set up with a view to a National Parliament to be convened in 1915. In the meantime the provincial councils were to elect an interim National Council.

The sudden demand for Western education was entirely beyond the supply of trained teachers. Mission colleges and schools were besieged with students ; and mandarins everywhere now besought mission schools for aid and for teachers. Tens of thousands of students flocked to Japan to receive there a veneer of education, a diploma, lowered morals, anti-foreign speeches and revolutionary notions.

Nevertheless reform progressed, schools and colleges of all kinds sprang up, and beneath a welter of inefficiency there was a determination to ' muddle through ' to better things. Let it not be thought that there was any increase in love for foreign nations. Rather the object of it all was to be rid of them, or at least to become their equal.

No greater proof of the moral and patriotic impulse can be given than the magnificent uprising against opium-smoking. The unceasing protests of missionaries and the gibes of the Japanese had produced their effect. Begun in 1906, the attack on the drug culminated in 1910, when the country was so far cleared of the drug that the British Government, on the advice of its able minister, Sir John Newell Jordan, consented to shorten the term previously agreed upon for the final cessation of the import from India.

In 1908 the Emperor died on November 15 and the Dowager the following day—a curious coincidence. His younger brother's infant son, who still lives as Emperor of the Manchus, was enthroned, with his father, Prince Chun, as regent. The Manchu dynasty began with a child and a regent, it ended with a child and a regent; but the first regent, Dorgun, was a man of discernment and power, the last regent was of another order. Every high office in Peking was soon filled with Manchu princes and nobles with sharp appetites for the spoils of office. Despite them, reform continued. The local and provincial councils were learning 'parliamentary methods, and the first National Assembly met in 1910.

XIV

REVOLUTION, REPUBLIC, RUIN, RENAISSANCE

SUDDENLY, from an apparently clear sky, burst an unseen cloud, which deluged the land, swept away the dynasty and thrust up a republic for which there had been no preparation. On Oct. 10, 1911, a bomb accidentally exploded in a secret revolutionary bomb factory at Hankow. The revolutionaries at once realized that they must take instant action or perish. They arose, put Colonel Li Yuan-hung (later president of the republic) at their head, and the revolution was at once in full swing. Students of all stages of youth flocked to its standards, even girl students forming fighting corps.

The Manchu regent, at the accession of his son to the throne, avenged his brother, the late emperor, by virtually dismissing from office his ablest viceroy, Yuan Shih-kai, for what he considered his treachery in 1898. Now, he had to recall him and entrust him with the crushing of the rebellion and the salvation of the dynasty. Ten out of the eighteen provinces had voted for a republic with Sun Yat-sen as president, and Nanking as the capital. The navy also had

declared for the revolution. Forty-six generals
of the northern army—probably encouraged by
Yuan Shih-k'ai—now demanded Manchu abdica-
tion, and on Feb. 11, 1912, that dynasty brought
its long and for the most part glorious reign to
an end, though the emperor still remained and
remains Emperor of the Manchus, till recently
occupying half of the palace, and receiving a
liberal pension.

The republic was now formally set up with
Yuan Shih-k'ai as first president, and with Sun
Yat-sen in a subsidiary office.

In the following year, 1913, Yuan's assumption
of a virtual dictatorship caused a serious disturbance, which he was, however, easily able to quell.
He was without doubt the man above all others
who could have given his country an orderly system
of government. Had he been content to remain
as president of the republic, and to have brought
into order a system of parliamentary government,
he would have gone down in history universally
honoured. Instead, at the end of 1915, he made
all arrangements to declare himself monarch
and the founder of a new dynasty. At first
everything seemed favourable ; but soon so great
was the storm raised throughout the country
that he had to annul his proposal. Chagrin and
anxiety overwhelmed him and he died on June 6,
1916.

Yuan's death left the country leaderless.
During the revolution the provinces had fallen

into the hands of military governors. The Central Government had never fully regained control over them. The politicians of the provinces had demanded provincial autonomy, and the military governors themselves took possession of it. Of these autocratic governors, recognizing no authority above them, only a few seem to possess a sense of honour or of patriotism, the majority seeking only their own advantage, at whatever cost to the suffering people.

The result at present is ruin. The republicans saw in the overthrow of the Manchus the arrival of the millenium. To them the Manchus were the enemies of all progress. If so, were they any worse than the Chinese officials? To suppose that the Chinese have been ruled and oppressed by an alien people, the Manchus, is only partly true. In fact, the vast majority of officials were always Chinese, not Manchus, and the Manchus in high places were no more anti-foreign and anti-progressive than were the Chinese in similar profitable places. He must be a hardy man who would charge the Manchus with responsibility for the ruin and chaos at present existing, for the military governors and all connected with them are Chinese. The marauding armies are Chinese, the bandits and pirates are Chinese, the officials, civil and military, are Chinese. In the south, ruin has been poured over the three provinces of Kuangtung, Kuangsi, and Fukien. As to the rest, there are only three or four provinces

where peace and prosperity prevail. Manchuria
is better ruled than most of the Chinese provinces,
and Chekiang and Shansi are up to the present
the two best ruled in China.

What of the future ? That China will some
day contain a great, prosperous and enlightened
people there can be no doubt. By what process
a renaissance will be brought about is far from
clear. The revolution was unnecessary and harm-
ful. Absolutely unprepared for the inevitable
result, without a Cromwell or a Washington, the
new rulers have enthroned chaos, with consequent
misery to the people. A constitutional monarchy
was the political principle of K'ang Yu-wei. His
own haste and the Empress Dowager ruined that
proposal. Will it be revived ? It may, but the
only available monarch is the youthful Manchu
Emperor, and his throne would be of dynamite.
Were a man of really noble mould to appear he
would not need a throne. No such man is in
sight. A great military genius might crush the
military governors one by one, but General
Wu P'ei-fu has failed. Another hope is the rise
of parliament and its alliance with a strong
military leader—but parliamentary votes have
been at the disposal of the highest bidder, openly
and blatantly. A ' purge ' was needed and made,
with what result is not yet manifest. Foreign
intervention might be the most rapid and effective
method of producing peace, but it would probably
drive all the Chinese generals into a unison of

resistance as it did in Russia. Moreover, Europe has more than enough difficulties of its own, and has no wish to be drawn into further responsibilities.

There is one institution, of which China is a member, of character neither European nor Asiatic, but international and inter-racial, which might be of service. It has the finest and most disinterested judges and statesmen of all races at its disposal, detached from all personal or national avidity. The League of Nations, if appealed to, might yet be able to induce the present war-lords to combine their personal ambitions in a larger one—the salvation of their country.

Ninety-nine per cent. of the people care only that goverament should give them security to toil untiringly for a bare living, and to bring up their families to a similar life of hard but willing labour. It is little they ask. Far more can be given them, if their leaders will but pool heart and brain for their welfare; in the end to their own enrichment.

The need of China is a new soul in her men of capacity. She has millions willing to die for her, but few in high places willing with single mind to live for her. Corruption, intrigue, personal ambition may be tolerated for a time in a clever leader, who uses these vices successfully for the benefit of the nation; but mediocre men, who are at the same time dishonest—men who for their country would sacrifice the whole but not the part, their life but not their greed—such men are useless as patriots.

That the renaissance will come is certain. In the meantime millions may have to die of famine, be plundered by soldiers, brigands, and pirates, and be oppressed by monstrous ill-government— and these millions are the most industrious, most thrifty, most easily governed people in the world.

XV

EAST AND WEST

EAST sought West and West sought East. It was destined the twain should meet. They each had ideas and commodities to share. They have met and are sharing them. Friction was the inevitable result. How to ease the friction and live together in a shrinking world is the present problem. Other means than those of force must be evolved. It is the office of men of reason, of goodwill and of large statesmanship to discover and apply them.

Has China unfriendly feelings towards the West? There is a measure of justification for them. But, if such unfriendliness has not been mutually helpful in the past, neither does it promise to be of help in the future. The difficulties are immense for all concerned. They would only be increased by the cultivation of animosity. Whether we like it or not, the nineteenth century has brought East and West to each other's doors. We are no longer strangers, with all the uncouth notions produced by tribal prejudice. We are neighbours, and must answer the question 'Who is my neighbour?' with a wider definition.

195

One of the most remarkable features of the
nineteenth century has been that of colonization.
It has not been limited to European expansion
overseas.   Steamships are democratic, and their
owners anxious to carry passengers of all tribes
and nations, as well as their goods.   For instance,
British ships under British officers serve thousands
of Moslem pilgrims, carrying them on their
journey to Mecca from places as distant as Java.
In like manner they have served large numbers
of colonists from Asia to other parts of the
world, and yearly they increase.   Not the least,
indeed perhaps the most enterprising of these
venturers abroad, are the Chinese.

Neither East nor West has perhaps yet fully
realized how willing the Chinese are to leave home
and become colonists.   Not only have they gone
in immense numbers to Manchuria and Mongolia,
but probably some ten millions of them are
dwelling in foreign territory.   Were such an insane
idea as a mutual exclusion act to be passed, East
and West, then for every European deported from
China, 350 Chinese would have to be deported
from their present foreign abodes.   Moreover,
Chinese emigration is steadily increasing, and
with four hundred millions of prolific people as
a basis there will be no lack of willing emigrants.
From Peru with its 45,000 Chinese to Java with
its two millions, from Siberia to Australia, each
with its 40,000, the Chinese are scattered all over
the world and in every land.   The part played

in France, during and after the war, by the hundred thousand Chinese workers calls for no reminder.

For two thousand years the Chinese have traded abroad, with the inevitable result of the formation of trading colonies. It is therefore as useless for a Chinese to ask a foreigner, ' Why did you foreigners come to China ? ' as it would be for the latter to ask a Chinese, ' Why have your people gone abroad ? ' For more than fifteen hundred years the Chinese have traded southward all down the Pacific coast, into the equatorial regions, as well as into the Indian Ocean, seeking ' spices ' as did the West. They have traded westward across the desert and the salt marsh, strewing both with their bones. For most of that time there have been Chinese colonies in all these directions. Far from being unwilling to live abroad, they have for many centuries had numerous settlements, large and small, all over eastern and central Asia. To-day they are, as ever, able, willing, and ready to ' inherit the earth,' and wherever they go are prepared to work diligently to develop it.

That is one of the difficulties which faces the people who possess the still empty spaces, and who are erecting barriers against the poverty, industry, and terrible prolificness of the Far East. The British Colonies have received what they rightly or wrongly consider to be their fair proportion. The United States of America takes a like attitude, and is now putting a severe limit even on European emigrants. Both nations have already serious problems of increasing native populations to face within their own territories.

This does not necessarily imply that there is any unfriendly feeling towards the Chinese. On the contrary, from the United States and from Great Britain as well as from various European countries, thousands of voluntary workers have gone to China for medical, educational and philanthropic purposes, one of their chief objects being to develop more human relations between East and West. These men and women seek to discover a common ground for future inter-racial harmony and co-operation in human welfare and relationship. They are the pioneers in studying the larger racial issues. They think the world can be made better for all, and aim at inducing all races to take their proper share in the process by bringing their contribution to the common-wealth of nations. The difficulty of their task is only equalled by its manifest importance.

Nor have they been without encouragement, for already they have influenced governments to realize the human side of affairs, national and racial. Their voice it was, for instance, which led the United States Government to favour the reception of Chinese students into American colleges, made possible by the remission of Boxer indemnity funds. Educated men and women from the United States and Great Britain were the pioneers, without fee or reward, in modern medicine and surgery in China, as well as in modern education for men and women.

It is from contact with the West that China has been awakened to a new life and a new environment, into which it naturally has some difficulty of adjustment. One thing may be accepted as axiomatic—it can never again live in isolation. The West is largely responsible. The West must be patient—not unmindful of its own difficulties. The East ought to be grateful. It is not—as yet. Men seldom are grateful for being aroused from a deep sleep. But the world is no longer flat and still. It is round and moves ; so China must move with it. It is a law of evolution which none of us can escape. Movement is life, stagnation death—and it is well to be good-tempered about it.

Steamships and railways are linking up China with itself and with the outside world. Modern posts, telegraphs, telephones, are spread over the land and stretching their fingers around the earth. The printing press with its books and newspapers has become a tremendous power for good and for ill. The modern mine and factory have come to stay, with the good and evil which always accompany industrial revolution. The whole political system of the country has been cast in an American mould. Just laws, as yet imperfectly administered, have been promulgated, bringing China into prospective line with the more advanced nations. The intellectual development of its masses, male and female equally, is now the distant goal to which scholars raise their eyes. Woman has been set upon her feet in more ways than one. Not least, the superstitious character of popular religion has been unveiled and a desire stimulated for some higher form of spirituality which can find expression in moral and social advancement, as well as directly in awe, adoration and gratitude. All these and more result from the contact of West with East.

Nor has the contribution been on one side only. If the West has carried its books to China, it was from there it obtained the idea of paper-making and probably of printing. If the West has taken its modern fabrications of 'silk,' it was from China that it learned its first lesson. If the West has taken its art to the East, it has received an equal gift in return. If it be true that China invented the compass, then the Chinese can hardly complain against other nations for being drawn by it to their coasts. But why proceed further ?

The lesson of it all seems clear—that the Power which made the nations, and which made the mountains with passes and the ocean for ships, meant also that nations should not dwell in separate worlds, but exchange commodities material and spiritual. How to live together for each other's welfare—that is the problem. Let East and West solve it together in a spirit of goodwill.

INDEX

Adams, John Quincey, 132.
Adams, William, 66.
Africa, 2, 9, 16, 25, 31, 60, 62, 78 ;
  Chinese in, 204.
Aglen, Sir Francis, 58.
Alcock, Sir Rutherford, 156-7.
Alexander the Great, 16, 20.
Alexandria, 16.
Allen, Dr. Young J., 173-6.
Allies, The : French and British,
  148-51 ; relieve Legations,
  184.
America, *see* U.S.A.
Amherst, Lord, 100-4, 152.
Amoy, 69, 71, 113, 134, 172 ;
  a Treaty Port, 135, 144, 208.
Amur River, 36, 185.
Annam, 7, 23, 28, 46 ; Franco-
  Chinese War, 161; Chinese in,
  204.
Anti-foreign feeling, 109, 158, 162,
  167, 182, 186, 191, 195.
Arabia, 24, 31, 62.
Arabs, 23-6, 28, 35, 46, 112.
Army, Chinese, 201.
Arrow War, 144, 147-151, 167.
Art, Buddhist, 17, 20, 21 ; of
  T'ang dynasty, 32.
Asia, Central, 1, 6, 8, 12, 14, 17,
  18, 20, 27, 31, 39, 54, 57, 62,
  197 ; Western, 9, 17, 30,
  38, 43, 46.
Astronomy, 2, 16, 27, 46, 91-3.
Attila, 36, 40.
Augustins, 83, 90.
Australia, Chinese in, 196, 204.
Austria, 41, 88, 168.
Aviation, 201.

Babylonian civilization, 1.
Bacon, Roger, 43.
Bactria, 8, 11, 16, 20.
Baghdad, 55.
Baikal Lake, 36.
Banditry, 191.

Baptist Missionary Society, 173.
' Barbarians,' Foreign, 99, 102,
  106-10, 120, 123, 132, 145,
  167, 176.
Belgium, 173.
Bengal, 58, 76.
Bokhara, 11, 12, 63.
Borneo, 55.
Boxer Rising, 165, 170-85 ; In-
  demnity, 198, 203.
Britain, Great ; British, 3, 14, 80,
  84, 87, 96-111, 136, 143-5 ;
  Arrow War, 147-51 ; Colleges,
  203 ; Consuls, 145, 181 ;
  Early travellers, 63-74 ;
  Government and policy, 72,
  96, 105-6, 122, 125, 128,
  130-1, 134 ; Korea, 185 ;
  Missionaries, 98, 149, 173,
  182, 198-9 ; Opium, 113-36,
  187 ; Population in China,
  207 ; Port Hamilton, 163 ;
  Russia, agreement with, 172 ;
  Taiping rebellion, 142 ;
  Trade, early, 96-111 ; Trade
  policy, 171 ; Wei-hai-wei,
  164-5, 171 ; Wireless, 208 ;
  Yang-tze ' sphere,' 168, 172.
Brown, Sir John Macleary, 153.
Buddha, 19, 20.
Buddhism, Buddhist, 11, 19, 20,
  22, 28-30, 44, 45, 57, 91 ;
  Art, 17, 20, 21 ; Sutra, 28.
Burma, 7, 17, 31, 49, 58, 160 ;
  Chinese in, 204.

Cabot, John, 62, 63.
Caliph, Omar, 28 ; Othman, 28 ;
  of Baghdad, 42.
Cambaluc, *see* Peking, names for.
Cambodia, 55, 58, 66, 76.
Camoens, 82.
Canada, Chinese in, 204.
Cannon, Founding of, 92.
Cantlie, Sir James, 175.

INDEX

INDEX

INDEX

INDEX

INDEX